Global Forum on Transparency and Exchange of Information for Tax Purposes Peer Reviews: Hong Kong, China 2013

PHASE 2:
IMPLEMENTATION OF THE STANDARD IN PRACTICE

November 2013
(reflecting the legal and regulatory framework
as at August 2013)

OECD
BETTER POLICIES FOR BETTER LIVES

This work is published on the responsibility of the Secretary-General of the OECD. The opinions expressed and arguments employed herein do not necessarily reflect the official views of the OECD or of the governments of its member countries or those of the Global Forum on Transparency and Exchange of Information for Tax Purposes.

This document and any map included herein are without prejudice to the status of or sovereignty over any territory, to the delimitation of international frontiers and boundaries and to the name of any territory, city or area.

Please cite this publication as:
OECD (2013), *Global Forum on Transparency and Exchange of Information for Tax Purposes Peer Reviews: Hong Kong, China 2013: Phase 2: Implementation of the Standard in Practice*, OECD Publishing.
http://dx.doi.org/10.1787/9789264206137-en

ISBN 978-92-64-20612-0 (print)
ISBN 978-92-64-20613-7 (PDF)

Series: Global Forum on Transparency and Exchange of Information for Tax Purposes Peer Reviews
ISSN 2219-4681 (print)
ISSN 2219-469X (online)

Corrigenda to OECD publications may be found on line at: *www.oecd.org/publishing/corrigenda*.

Table of Contents

About the Global Forum

The Global Forum on Transparency and Exchange of Information for Tax Purposes is the multilateral framework within which work in the area of tax transparency and exchange of information is carried out by over 120 jurisdictions, which participate in the Global Forum on an equal footing.

The Global Forum is charged with in-depth monitoring and peer review of the implementation of the international standards of transparency and exchange of information for tax purposes. These standards are primarily reflected in the 2002 OECD *Model Agreement on Exchange of Information on Tax Matters* and its commentary, and in Article 26 of the OECD *Model Tax Convention on Income and on Capital* and its commentary as updated in 2004. The standards have also been incorporated into the UN *Model Tax Convention.*

The standards provide for international exchange on request of foreseeably relevant information for the administration or enforcement of the domestic tax laws of a requesting party. Fishing expeditions are not authorised but all foreseeably relevant information must be provided, including bank information and information held by fiduciaries, regardless of the existence of a domestic tax interest.

All members of the Global Forum, as well as jurisdictions identified by the Global Forum as relevant to its work, are being reviewed. This process is undertaken in two phases. Phase 1 reviews assess the quality of a jurisdiction's legal and regulatory framework for the exchange of information, while Phase 2 reviews look at the practical implementation of that framework. Some Global Forum members are undergoing combined – Phase 1 and Phase 2 – reviews. The Global Forum has also put in place a process for supplementary reports to follow-up on recommendations, as well as for the ongoing monitoring of jurisdictions following the conclusion of a review. The ultimate goal is to help jurisdictions to effectively implement the international standards of transparency and exchange of information for tax purposes.

All review reports are published once adopted by the Global Forum.

For more information on the work of the Global Forum on Transparency and Exchange of Information for Tax Purposes, and for copies of the published review reports, please refer to www.oecd.org/tax/transparency and www.eoi-tax.org.

Executive Summary

1. This report summarises the legal and regulatory framework for transparency and exchange of information in the Hong Kong Special Administrative Region of the People's Republic of China (hereinafter "Hong Kong") as well as the practical implementation of that framework. The assessment of effectiveness in practice has been performed in relation to a three-year period (1 July 2009 to 30 June 2012).

2. Hong Kong is a major international financial centre and a highly developed economy. It is an important source of the People's Republic of China (PRC)'s foreign direct investment inflow. Hong Kong has an integrated network of institutions and markets, which provide a wide range of products and services to local and international customers and investors. As such, Hong Kong has been supportive of efforts by the international community to promote transparency in tax administration. In 2005, Hong Kong committed to the internationally agreed standard for international exchange of information (EOI) in tax matters.

3. In February 2009, the Financial Secretary of Hong Kong announced the Government's decision to put forward legislative amendments to lift the domestic tax interest requirement. The legislative amendments came into operation in March 2010 and enabled Hong Kong's competent authority to access information for EOI purposes without a domestic tax interest. Following this legislative amendment, Hong Kong has actively sought to update and extend its EOI network, signing 26 agreements or protocols incorporating the internationally agreed standard for EOI. In addition, Hong Kong has 10 treaty negotiations in various stages of progress. Hong Kong authorities report that they have been in contact with approximately 14 other jurisdictions, including OECD members, G20 members and major trading partners, to explore the possibility of commencing treaty negotiations with an exchange of information article to the internationally agreed standard.

4. Hong Kong's legal and regulatory framework generally ensures that accurate, adequate and reasonably current information concerning legal ownership and control of companies, partnerships, and trusts is maintained in Hong Kong. Bank information and accounting records, including underlying

documentation, are also required to be maintained. However, some improvements are needed to Hong Kong's legal and regulatory framework to ensure effective EOI, notably with respect to the availability of ownership and identity information of owners of share warrants to bearer, companies where shares are held by nominees, and private express trusts with respect to which a trustee is resident in Hong Kong. With respect to share warrants to bearer, the new *Companies Ordinance*, which has been enacted on 10 August 2012 but is not yet in operation, repeals the power of a company to issue these warrants.

5. Compliance with all entities' obligations to maintain ownership, accounting and banking information is monitored by the Inland Revenue Department, the Companies Registry and other public authorities, such as the Hong Kong Monetary Authority and the Securities and Futures Commission. Sanctions are set at the appropriate level to ensure compliance with information keeping requirements and such sanctions are regularly enforced in practice. According to the feedback received from Hong Kong's EOI partners, no issues have arisen with respect to obtaining ownership, accounting or banking information during the three-year period under review.

6. As a result of the legislative amendments to the *Inland Revenue Ordinance* in 2010, Hong Kong's tax authorities have extensive powers to access bank, ownership, identity and accounting records absent a domestic tax interest and have measures to compel the production of such information for EOI purposes. For the three agreements signed before the passage of these amendments, Hong Kong requires a domestic tax interest in the matter in order to exercise these powers. Hong Kong's competent authority reports that it has been in contact with these jurisdictions on a number of occasions in order to update the respective agreements in line with the standard. Hong Kong has no domestic law restrictions based on dual criminality or bank secrecy rules. Rights and safeguards (e.g. notification, appeal rights) in Hong Kong do not restrict or delay effective EOI in practice.

7. Administration of the EOI articles under Hong Kong's treaty network is the responsibility of Hong Kong's competent authority, being the Commissioner of Inland Revenue. Hong Kong has signed 29 double taxation conventions (DTCs), 26 of which meet the internationally agreed standard. Twenty-two of Hong Kong's DTCs that meet the standard are currently in force. The ratification process for one additional DTC that meets the standard has been completed in Hong Kong.

8. Hong Kong has signed agreements that meet the international standard with eight of its most significant trading partners, seven of which are in force, and has signed agreements with a number of other economically significant jurisdictions. Some jurisdictions have approached Hong Kong on a number of occasions to negotiate tax information exchange agreements (TIEAs) without success, as Hong Kong was at that time unable to enter into such agreements. Hong Kong's laws have been amended recently and

now allow for the establishment of TIEAs. As a result, Hong Kong is now in a position to negotiate and enter into TIEAs with its relevant partners. It is recommended that Hong Kong do so expeditiously and ensure that all its relevant EOI partners have access to full exchange of information.

9. Hong Kong has gained practical experience with exchanging information over the years. Most of the EOI requests received by Hong Kong to date have come from Hong Kong's main trading partner, the PRC. Given the entry into force of a number of EOI agreements in recent years, including EOI agreements with major trading partners, and the continued expansion of Hong Kong's EOI network, the number of incoming EOI requests has started to increase.

10. Hong Kong's competent authority is well prepared to deal with increasing demand and has adequate resources to exchange information effectively. There is a sufficient number of professional staff with clear responsibility for processing requests and retrieving or obtaining the requested information. The staff members also possess the requisite expertise and have undergone training specific to international EOI. Comprehensive guidelines have been issued covering all relevant steps in the EOI process. Following the entry into force of the new legislation, Hong Kong's policies and practices with respect to the temporal scope of application of treaties have been adjusted to meet the international standards.

11. Inputs received from Hong Kong's peers confirm that Hong Kong's EOI practices are adequate and they consider Hong Kong to be an efficient and co-operative partner. Out of 61 incoming requests on direct taxation matters received from 1 July 2009 to 30 June 2012, Hong Kong answered 75% of the cases within 90 days, and 85% within 180 days. In relation to two complex cases, Hong Kong took more than one year to furnish a reply (responses were provided within 15 months). Peer jurisdictions were satisfied with the timeliness and the content of the responses received.

12. Hong Kong has been assigned a rating[1] for each of the 10 essential elements as well as an overall rating. The ratings for the essential elements are based on the analysis in the text of the report, taking into account the Phase 1 determinations and any recommendations made in respect of Hong Kong's legal and regulatory framework and the effectiveness of its exchange of information in practice. On this basis, Hong Kong has been assigned the following ratings: Compliant for elements A.3, B.1, B.2, C.3, C.4 and C.5, Largely Compliant for elements A.2 and C.1 and Partially Compliant for elements A.1 and C.2. In view of the ratings for each of the essential elements taken in their entirety, the overall rating for Hong Kong is Largely Compliant.

1. This report reflects the legal and regulatory framework as at the date indicated on page 1 of this publication. Any material changes to the circumstances affecting the ratings may be included in Annex 1 to this report.

13. A follow up report on the steps undertaken by Hong Kong to answer the recommendations made in this report should be provided to the PRG within twelve months of the adoption of this report.

Introduction

Information and methodology used for the peer review of Hong Kong, China

14. The assessment of the legal and regulatory framework of Hong Kong and the practical implementation and effectiveness of this framework was based on the international standards for transparency and exchange of information as described in the Global Forum's *Terms of Reference to Monitor and Review Progress Towards Transparency and Exchange of Information For Tax Purposes*, and was prepared using the Global Forum's *Methodology for Peer Reviews and Non-Member Reviews.*

15. The assessment has been conducted in two stages: Phase 1, carried out in 2011, and Phase 2, carried out in 2013.

16. The 2011 Phase 1 Report of Hong Kong, which was adopted and published by the Global Forum in October 2011, was based on the laws, regulations, and EOI mechanisms in force or effect as at 19 August 2011, other materials supplied by Hong Kong, and information supplied by partner jurisdictions.

17. The Phase 2 assessment looked at the practical implementation of Hong Kong's legal framework, as well as any amendments made to the legal and regulatory framework since the Phase 1 review. The assessment was based on the laws, regulations, and EOI mechanisms in force or effect as at 19 August 2013. It also reflects Hong Kong's responses to the Phase 1 and Phase 2 questionnaires, other information, explanations and materials supplied by Hong Kong during and after the Phase 2 on-site visit that took place in Hong Kong from 5 to 7 March 2013 and information supplied by partner jurisdictions. During the on-site visit, the assessment team met with officials and representatives of Hong Kong's Inland Revenue Department, Financial Services and the Treasury Bureau, Business Registration Office, Companies Registry, Department of Justice, Securities and Futures Commission, Hong Kong Monetary Authority, The Law Society of Hong Kong, the Hong Kong Institute of Certified Public Accountants, Hong Kong Trustees' Association and Hong Kong Institute of Chartered Secretaries. A list of all those interviewed during the onsite visit is attached to this report at Annex 4.

18. The following analysis reflects the Phase 1 and Phase 2 assessments of the legal and regulatory framework of Hong Kong in effect as at 19 August 2013 and the practical implementation and effectiveness of this framework during the three-year review period of 1 July 2009 to 30 June 2012.

19. The Terms of Reference break down the standards of transparency and exchange of information into 10 essential elements and 31 enumerated aspects under three broad categories: (A) availability of information; (B) access to information; and (C) exchanging information. This review assesses Hong Kong's legal and regulatory framework and the implementation and effectiveness of this framework against these elements and each of the enumerated aspects. In respect of each essential element a determination is made regarding Hong Kong's legal and regulatory framework that either: *(i)* the element is in place, *(ii)* the element is in place but certain aspects of the legal implementation of the element need improvement, or *(iii)* the element is not in place. These determinations are accompanied by recommendations for improvement where relevant. In addition, to reflect the Phase 2 component, recommendations are made concerning Hong Kong's practical application of each of the essential elements and a rating of either: *(i)* compliant, *(ii)* largely compliant, *(iii)* partially compliant, or *(iv)* non-compliant is assigned to each element. An overall rating is also assigned to reflect Hong Kong's overall level of compliance with the standards.

20. The Phase 1 and Phase 2 assessments were conducted by teams comprising expert assessors and representatives of the Global Forum Secretariat. For the Phase 1 assessment, these were: Ms. Aislinn Walwyn of the Australian Taxation Office; Ms. Tímea Borók of the Hungarian Division of International Taxation; and Mr. Stewart Brant from the Global Forum Secretariat. In the Phase 2 assessment, the assessment team comprised Ms. Aislinn Walwyn of the Australian Taxation Office; Ms. Tímea Borók of the Hungarian Division of International Taxation; and Ms. Renata Teixeira from the Global Forum Secretariat.

21. The ratings assigned in this report were adopted by the Global Forum in November 2013 as part of a comparative exercise designed to ensure the consistency of the results. An expert team of assessors was selected to propose ratings for a representative subset of 50 jurisdictions. Consequently, the assessment teams that carried out the Phase 1 and Phase 2 reviews were not involved in the assignment of ratings. These ratings have been compared with the ratings assigned to other jurisdictions for each of the essential elements to ensure a consistent and comprehensive approach.

Overview of Hong Kong, China

22. Hong Kong is a Special Administrative Region of the People's Republic of China (PRC). Following British rule from 1842 to 1997, the PRC assumed sovereignty under the "one country, two systems" principle. Hong Kong's constitutional document, the *Basic Law*, ensures that the current political situation will remain in effect for 50 years.

23. Hong Kong is located on the south-eastern tip of China and covers Hong Kong Island, Lantau Island, the Kowloon Peninsula and the New Territories, including 262 outlying islands. Hong Kong has an area of 1 100 square kilometres and a population of approximately 7 million.[2] Hong Kong is one of the most densely populated places in the world. The land population density stood at 6 480 persons per square kilometre in 2010 and remained at similar levels in 2012. People of Chinese descent comprise the vast majority of the population, with foreign nationals comprising 5%. English and Chinese are Hong Kong's official languages. The Cantonese dialect is the most commonly spoken version of Chinese in the territory.

24. Hong Kong's economy is characterised by free trade, low taxation and minimum government intervention. It is the world's 9th largest trading economy in merchandise trade in 2012, with the PRC as its most significant trading partner. In 2012, Hong Kong's other major trading partners were, in order of significance: the United States, Japan, Chinese Taipei, Singapore, the Republic of Korea, India, Germany, Thailand, Malaysia, the United Kingdom, Switzerland, Vietnam, France, Italy, the United Arab Emirates, the Netherlands, the Philippines, Australia and Belgium. 3 Hong Kong's gross domestic product (GDP) was HKD 2 040 billion (EUR 201.4 billion) in 2012. The Hong Kong dollar (HKD) is Hong Kong's currency. As at 20 April 2013, HKD 10.13= EUR 1.[4]

General information on legal system and the taxation system

25. Hong Kong's legal system is based on the rule of law and the independence of the judiciary. The constitutional framework is provided by the *Basic Law*. The *Basic Law* was enacted by the National People's Congress in accordance with the *Constitution* of the PRC. It is akin to a mini-constitution for Hong Kong. It was promulgated on 4 April 1990 and took effect on 1 July 1997 on the transfer of sovereignty over Hong Kong from the United Kingdom to the PRC. All the systems and policies practised in Hong Kong are based on

2. Statistics Hong Kong, www.censtatd.gov.hk/hong_kong_statistics/statistics_by_subject/index.jsp, accessed 22 June 2011.
3. Hong Kong's Principal Trading Partners in 2012, www.tid.gov.hk/english/trade_relations/mainland/trade.html, accessed on 25 July 2013.
4. www.xe.com/, accessed 20 April 2013.

the provisions of the *Basic Law.* These include the social and economic systems; the system for safeguarding the fundamental rights and freedoms of its residents; the executive, legislative and judicial systems; and relevant policies. No law enacted by the legislature of Hong Kong may contravene the *Basic Law.*

26. Under the *Basic Law*, all the laws previously in force in Hong Kong (that is, the common law, rules of equity, ordinances, subordinate legislation and customary law) are maintained, subject to any amendment by Hong Kong's legislature, except for any that contravene the *Basic Law.* National laws of the PRC are not applied in Hong Kong except for a number of such laws relating to defence and foreign affairs, which are listed in Annex III to the *Basic Law.*

27. The *Basic Law* details the fundamental rights, freedoms and duties of the residents of Hong Kong. These rights include the right to equality before the law; freedom of speech, of the press and of publication; freedom of association, of assembly, of procession and of demonstration; and the right and freedom to form and join trade unions, and to strike; freedom of movement; freedom of conscience; and freedom of religious belief.

28. The *Basic Law* has the highest status in the hierarchy of law of Hong Kong. Under Article 17 of the *Basic Law*, Hong Kong is vested with legislative power. Laws enacted by the legislature of Hong Kong must be reported to the Standing Committee of the National People's Congress for record. Under Article 73, the Legislative Council of Hong Kong exercises the powers and functions to enact, amend or repeal laws in accordance with the provisions of the *Basic Law* and legal procedures. Subsidiary legislation may be made under delegated powers granted by primary legislation made by the Legislative Council of Hong Kong. A piece of subsidiary legislation may not be inconsistent with the primary legislation pursuant to which the subsidiary legislation was enacted in the first place. Treaties do not automatically have the force of law in Hong Kong and have to be implemented by way of enactment as pieces of domestic law. Accordingly, treaties do not *per se* override domestic law where there is conflict between the two. Any conflict between domestic law reflecting treaty contents and other domestic law will be resolved in accordance with statutory interpretation principles.

29. Under Article 13(3) of the *Basic Law*, the Central People's Government authorises Hong Kong to conduct relevant external affairs on its own in accordance with the *Basic Law.* Under Article 151, Hong Kong may, on its own, conclude and implement agreements with foreign states and regions and relevant international organisations in areas including the economic, trade, financial and monetary, shipping, communications, tourism, cultural and sports fields. On this basis, Hong Kong may conclude agreements with foreign states and regions on the avoidance of double taxation.

30. The major courts in Hong Kong include the Magistrates' Courts, the District Court (includes the Family Court), the High Court (comprises the Court of First Instance and the Court of Appeal) and the Court of Final Appeal which is the highest appellate court in Hong Kong. The judiciary is responsible for the administration of justice in Hong Kong. It hears all prosecutions and civil disputes (including tax disputes).

The tax system

31. The *Inland Revenue Ordinance* (Cap.112) governs the taxation of individuals, corporations, partnerships, sole-proprietorships or trustees, whether incorporated or unincorporated. This ordinance provides for the levying of three separate direct taxes in Hong Kong: profits tax, salaries tax, and property tax. The standard tax rate is 15% for salaries tax, property tax, and profits tax for unincorporated businesses, while the profits tax rate for corporations is 16.5%. There is no capital gains tax or value added tax in Hong Kong. There is no withholding tax levied on dividends or interest. Generally, dividends are not deductible, whereas interest is, but subject to certain anti-avoidance provisions. Royalties and fees paid to non-resident entertainers or sportsmen for their performance in Hong Kong are subject to withholding tax on their assessable profits charged under profits tax.

32. Hong Kong's tax system adopts the "territorial principle", i.e. taxes are only levied on income derived from or arising in Hong Kong and not on income sourced outside Hong Kong. The *Inland Revenue Ordinance* contains no exemption from profits tax for non-Hong Kong companies. Since Hong Kong applies a territorial basis of assessment, liability to tax is determined not on residence status, but on the source of income.

33. Profits tax is levied on corporations, partnerships, and trustees. Whether a company is liable to profits tax depends on the nature and extent of its activities in Hong Kong. The following conditions must be satisfied for a profits tax liability: the person must carry on a trade, profession or business in Hong Kong; the profits to be charged must be from such trade, profession or business carried on by the person in Hong Kong; and the profits must be profits arising in or derived from Hong Kong. No tax is levied on profits arising abroad, even if they are remitted to Hong Kong.

34. The term "trade" is defined in section 2(1) of the *Inland Revenue Ordinance* to include "every trade and manufacture and every adventure, and concern in the nature of trade". The term "business" is also defined in section 2(1) to include "the letting or sub-letting by any corporation to any person of any premises or portion thereof, and the sub-letting by any other person of any premises or portion of any premises held by him under a lease or tenancy

other than from the Government". The term "profession" is not defined and the ordinary meaning applies.

35. The question of whether a business is carried on in Hong Kong and whether profits are derived from Hong Kong is largely one of fact; however decisions of the Hong Kong Courts and the Privy Council indicate that there is a very low threshold for a person to carry on business in Hong Kong. In the case of a company incorporated for the purpose of making profits for its shareholders, any gainful use to which it puts any of its assets *prima facie* amounts to carrying on business.[5] The carrying on of business usually calls for some activity on the part of whoever carries it on, though, depending on the nature of the business, the activity may be intermittent with long intervals of quiescence in between. A company need not have extensive activities in Hong Kong before it is considered to be carrying on business in Hong Kong.

36. The income of a trust derived from a business carried on in Hong Kong is chargeable to profits tax. The income is chargeable in the name of the trustee as the definition of "person" in section 2(1) of the *Inland Revenue Ordinance* includes "trustee". Thus trustees, like other persons carrying on businesses in Hong Kong, are required to furnish profits tax returns with the Inland Revenue Department (IRD) and are bound by the various statutory requirements laid down in the *Inland Revenue Ordinance*.

37. Section 14 of the *Inland Revenue Ordinance* makes it clear that only profits arising in or derived from Hong Kong are chargeable to profits tax. Though the word "source" is not used in s. 14, it is accepted that the words "arising in or derived from" is equivalent to the concept of source. "Source" is not a legal concept, but a question of fact depending on the nature of the transaction. The broad guiding principle, enshrined in decisions of the Privy Council and Court of Final Appeal, is that "one looks to see what the tax-payer has done to earn the profit in question and where he or she has done it" (i.e. what were the operations which produced the relevant profits and where those operations took place).

38. The IRD issued Departmental Interpretation and Practice Note 21 on Locality of Profits (DIPN 21) to clarify issues regarding the source of profits. DIPN 21 provides that Hong Kong generally applies the "operations test", which involves identifying activities that are most important in generating the profits and the place at which these activities are carried out. For trading companies, all relevant operations carried out to earn the profits, including the solicitation of orders, negotiation, conclusion, trade financing, shipment and performance of contracts, would be considered. In the case of service companies, the place where the services are performed which give rise to the

5. *Commissioner of Inland Revenue v. Hang Seng Bank Limited* (1991); *Commissioner of Inland Revenue v Bartica Investment Ltd* (1996).

fees would be the determining factor. In respect of companies holding investment property, the location of the property is considered.

39. In support of a claim that profits are offshore in nature and not chargeable to profits tax, taxpayers are required to supply detailed documentary evidence to Hong Kong's tax authorities such as copies of contracts, purchase/sales orders, invoices, shipping documents, banking facilities letters, breakdown of suppliers and customers, *etc.* The IRD reports that tax authorities raise further queries and obtain further facts and documents from taxpayers before arriving at the decision as to whether their "offshore" claim can be accepted.

40. The *Inland Revenue Ordinance* is administered by the IRD. Apart from the three major taxes, the IRD also administers the *Business Registration Ordinance* (Cap.310) which governs the registration of businesses in Hong Kong.

International exchange of information for tax purposes

41. As an international financial centre and a fast developing economy, Hong Kong has been supportive of efforts by the international community to promote transparency in tax administration. In 2005, Hong Kong endorsed the Global Forum's principles of transparency and effective exchange of information. Since that time, Hong Kong's domestic laws have been amended to better align them with the standards.

42. Hong Kong's legal and regulatory framework relevant to EOI for tax purposes is presided over by the Financial Services and the Treasury Bureau. Administration of EOI under Hong Kong's treaty network is the responsibility of Hong Kong's competent authority, i.e. the Commissioner of Inland Revenue. The *Inland Revenue (Amendment) Ordinance 2010* and the *Inland Revenue (Disclosure of Information) Rules* (Cap.112BI), which came into operation on 12 March 2010, are the primary pieces of legislation permitting the IRD to exchange information under a DTC. Following the enactment of the *Inland Revenue (Amendment) (No. 2) Ordinance 2013* on 19 July 2013, the EOI under a TIEA is also allowed. Under the *Inland Revenue Ordinance,* the Commissioner or his authorised representatives are empowered to obtain ownership, identity, bank information and accounting records for the purpose of responding to a specific request for EOI in tax matters (s. 51).

43. As at 12 August 2013, Hong Kong is signatory to 26 agreements which provide EOI to the standard, of which 22 are currently in force. A complete list of the DTCs which have been concluded by Hong Kong is set out in Annex 2 to this report.

Overview of the financial sector and relevant professions

44. Hong Kong is a major international financial centre, comprising an integrated network of institutions and markets which provide a wide range of products and services to local and international customers and investors. The financial sector employs 230 000 people, or six per cent of Hong Kong's total workforce. It is a high value-added industry that contributes 16% to GDP.[6] Hong Kong's financial markets are characterised by a high degree of liquidity.

45. The principal regulators of Hong Kong's financial markets are the Hong Kong Monetary Authority (HKMA)[7], the Securities and Futures Commission, the Office of the Commissioner of Insurance and the Mandatory Provident Fund Schemes Authority. They are responsible respectively for regulation of the banking; securities and futures; and insurance and retirement scheme industries.

46. In the banking sector, there are 155 licensed banks, 21 restricted licence banks and 24 deposit-taking companies in Hong Kong, together with 60 local representative offices of overseas banking institutions (as at March 2013). These institutions are from 35 jurisdictions and include 70 out of the world's largest 100 banks. Together they operate a comprehensive network of approximately 1 391 local branches, excluding their principal place of business in Hong Kong. Banks in Hong Kong engage in a wide range of retail and wholesale banking business such as deposit-taking, trade financing, corporate finance, treasury activities, precious metal trading and securities broking.

47. The following three types of institutions are collectively known as "authorised institutions" in the *Banking Ordinance* (Cap.155) and are subject to the supervision of the HKMA:

- banks;
- restricted licence banks (principally engaged in merchant banking and capital market activities. They may take deposits of any maturity of HKD 500 000 (EUR 49 358) and above); and
- deposit-taking companies (mostly owned by banks. These companies engage in a range of specialised activities, including consumer finance and securities business. They may take deposits of HKD 100 000

6. The 2013-14 Budget speech available at www.budget.gov.hk/2013/eng/speech.html, accessed on 29 April 2013.
7. Besides banking supervision, the HKMA is also responsible for maintenance of currency stability and promotion of the efficiency, integrity and development of Hong Kong's financial system.

(EUR 9 872) or above with an original term of maturity of at least three months).

48. The external net assets held by banks and deposit-taking institutions reached HKD 2 143 billion (EUR 211.5 billion) at the end of January 2013, making Hong Kong one of the largest banking centres in the world. Hong Kong's stock market was the sixth largest in the world and the second largest in Asia in terms of market capitalisation as at the end of September 2012.[8] The total value of fund assets under management in Hong Kong is more than HKD 9 trillion (EUR 0.9 trillion), ranking second in Asia.[9]

49. Hong Kong also has credit unions, which are co-operative organisations formed under the 1968 *Credit Union Ordinance* (Cap.119). As at 31 December 2012, there were 44 credit unions in Hong Kong. Over 98% of assets of credit unions belong to those formed by employees of government departments and large public and private corporations. They have a total membership of about 78 981 and a total share capital of HKD 8.7 billion (EUR 0.9 billion).

50. Money Service Operators (MSOs) provide international remittance and money exchange services. As at 28 February 2013, there were approximately 1 100 licensed MSOs in Hong Kong. MSOs are licensed under the *Anti-Money Laundering and Counter-Terrorist Financing (Financial Institutions) Ordinance* (Cap.615) which is in effect since 1 April 2012.

51. The *Insurance Companies Ordinance* (Cap.41) provides the legislative framework for the insurance industry. The Commissioner of Insurance, appointed by the Chief Executive of Hong Kong as the Insurance Authority, has the principal function under the *Insurance Companies Ordinance* to regulate and supervise the insurance industry so as to promote its general stability and protect policy holders. As at 28 February 2013, there were 155 authorised insurers in Hong Kong engaging in different types of business i.e. long-term (e.g. individual life, retirement scheme management), general (e.g. accident and health, property damage) and composite.

52. Firms engaged in the securities and futures industry (licensed corporations) are supervised and regulated by the Securities and Futures Commission, an autonomous statutory body under the *Securities and Futures Ordinance* (Cap.571). As at 31 December 2012, there were 1 897 licensed corporations. The securities and futures markets are operated by the Hong Kong Exchanges and Clearing Limited. A wide variety of products are traded on the Hong Kong

---

8. www.gov.hk/en/about/abouthk/factsheets/docs/financial_services.pdf, accessed on 28 June 2013.
9. The 2013-14 Budget speech available at www.budget.gov.hk/2013/eng/speech.html, assessed on 29 April 2013.

Futures Exchange or the Stock Exchange of Hong Kong. As at April 2013, 20 overseas exchanges and market operators were authorised to offer their trading services to institutions in Hong Kong.

53. Hong Kong is a major asset management centre in Asia. According to a survey conducted by the Hong Kong Trustees' Association (HKTA) in 2012, as at the end of 2011, the trust sector managed assets estimated at HKD 2 600 billion (EUR 256.7 billion). The HKTA, established in 1991 by members of the trust and fiduciary services sectors, is the leading professional body representing this sector in Hong Kong.

54. The legal profession in Hong Kong is divided into two distinct branches – barristers (also known as "counsel") and solicitors, both regulated by the *Legal Practitioners Ordinance* (Cap.159). Solicitors have limited rights of audience before the courts whereas barristers have unlimited rights of audience in all courts and tribunals where legal representation is allowed. The Bar Council of the Hong Kong Bar Association is the governing body for barristers. The Law Society of Hong Kong is the governing body of the solicitors' profession. The total number of practising lawyers in Hong Kong is 8 655 (7 477 solicitors and 1 178 barristers).

55. The Hong Kong Institute of Certified Public Accountants, established under the *Professional Accountants Ordinance* (Cap.50), performs such functions as registration of and granting practising certificates to certified public accountants (CPAs), standard setting, handling complaints and disciplinary cases, and conducting practice reviews. It requires members to comply with its Code of Ethics for Professional Accountants (s. 430 of the Code of Ethics is specific to tax practice), failure of which may result in enquiry by the appropriate committee established under the authority of the Institute, as well as disciplinary action. As at 28 February 2013, there were 34 516 CPAs in Hong Kong.

56. The Hong Kong Institute of Chartered Secretaries is an independent professional body with approximately 5 700 members and 3 200 students. Approximately 2 300 are potentially engaged within the trust and company services sector. Of these, about 760 work in law firms and accounting firms and would thus also be regulated by the Law Society of Hong Kong or the Hong Kong Institute of Certified Public Accountants, as the case may be. The types of activities or businesses which chartered secretaries working as trust and company services providers typically engage in include: company formation and establishment of business; arranging for bank accounts to be opened and acting as bank account signatories; acting as nominee shareholders and directors; providing registered office facility; liquidation and dissolution of companies and cessation of business; and trust services.

Overview of the anti-money laundering/combating financing of terrorism framework (AML/CFT)

57. Hong Kong's AML/CFT regime is derived from a number of statutes: the *Anti-Money Laundering and Counter-Terrorist Financing (Financial Institutions) Ordinance* (AMLO), the *Drug Trafficking (Recovery of Proceeds) Ordinance*, the *Organized and Serious Crimes Ordinance* and the *United Nations (Anti-Terrorism Measures) Ordinance*. The *AMLO*, which came into effect on 1 April 2012, imposes requirements on financial institutions regarding customer due diligence and record-keeping, whereas the three other ordinances require reporting of suspicious transactions regarding money laundering or terrorist financing. Credit unions are exempt from customer due diligence requirements, as they were considered by the Hong Kong authorities to represent low AML/CFT risk, because membership of those entities is limited to persons having a common bond – usually based on employment or trade – and whose full identity information is screened when they apply for membership. Other requirements for credit unions to maintain relevant information are in place. In particular, section 15 of the Credit Union Ordinance (Cap. 119) requires every credit union to maintain identity records in respect of their members.

58. The Joint Financial Intelligence Unit (JFIU), jointly run by staff from the Hong Kong Police Force and the Hong Kong Customs & Excise Department, receives, analyses and stores suspicious transactions reports and disseminates them to the appropriate investigative units.

59. Hong Kong is a member of the Financial Action Task Force (FATF) and the Asia-Pacific Group on Money Laundering. The third mutual evaluation report of Hong Kong was adopted on 11 July 2008. After undergoing a follow up review, the FATF recognised that Hong Kong had made significant progress in implementing the FATF standards. This resulted in Hong Kong being removed from the "follow-up process".[10] Hong Kong will be subject to the next round of evaluation in 2016.

Recent developments

60. On 12 July 2012, a new *Companies Ordinance* was passed by Hong Kong's Legislative Council. The ordinance substantially revises the legal framework governing the incorporation and operation of companies in Hong Kong. The new *Companies Ordinance* was gazetted on 10 August 2012 and will "come into operation on a day to be appointed by the Secretary for Financial Services and the Treasury by notice published in the Gazette". It is expected that it will

10. See the Mutual Evaluation Report of Hong Kong, China – 4th Follow up report published in October 2012 www.fatf-gafi.org/media/fatf/documents/reports/Follow%20up%20report%20MER%20Hong%20Kong%20China.pdf (accessed on 8 April 2013).

come into operation in the first quarter of 2014, after the enactment of the necessary subsidiary legislation as indicated in the Companies Registry External Circular No. 5/2012. In parallel, the Companies Registry is working to enhance its information system and carry out an overall review of its procedures and forms for the implementation of the new legislation. The exact date of entry into force is not yet known. Significantly, the new *Companies Ordinance* will repeal the power of a company to issue share warrants to bearer, whilst imposing no obligation on holders of share warrants to bearer issued prior to its effective date to surrender their share warrant for cancellation.

61. On 19 July 2013, the *Inland Revenue (Amendment) (No. 2) Ordinance 2013* was enacted providing the legal framework for Hong Kong to enter into TIEAs. This ordinance, which takes effect from 19 July 2013, also clarifies that the IRD's access powers extend to information that is under a person's control, in addition to information that is in a person's possession. The law also permits the Commissioner of Inland Revenue to exchange information relating to the administration or enforcement of the tax laws of an EOI partner in respect of any period that starts after the EOI arrangement came into operation, even if that information pre-dates such period.

62. The *Trust Law (Amendment) Ordinance 2013*, providing for amendments to the legal framework governing Hong Kong trusts, was gazetted on 26 July 2013 and will come into force on 1 December 2013. The *Ordinance* provides for certain amendments to the *Trustee Ordinance* and *the Perpetuities and Accumulations Ordinance* to extend trustees' powers in certain respects; to impose a statutory duty of care on trustees; to provide for the validity of certain trusts; to abolish the rule against perpetuities; to change the rule against excessive accumulation of income. Subject to the terms of the trust instrument, the statutory duty of care will apply to trustees in exercising powers and duties when making investments, appointing agents, nominees and custodians, taking out insurance, etc. The default statutory duty of care, when it is applicable, will replace the existing common law duty of care which might otherwise apply. The statutory duty of care is default in nature, but is not mandatory. Settlors will be given flexibility to reflect their intention in the trust instrument (*i.e*, the duty can be excluded or modified by the trust instrument).

63. The Government of Hong Kong proposes allowing the establishment of Open-ended Investment Companies ("OEIC"), to operate and manage investment funds. Further details are not yet available as they are still being developed by the Hong Kong authorities.

64. Since its Phase 1 review in 2011, Hong Kong has significantly expanded its network of EOI instruments. It signed 10 additional DTCs/protocols and brought into force 16 others. DTC negotiations are in progress with 10 jurisdictions: Bahrain; Bangladesh; Finland; India; South Korea; Macao, China; Mauritius; Saudi Arabia; South Africa and the United Arab Emirates.

Compliance with the Standards

A. Availability of Information

Overview

65. Effective exchange of information requires the availability of reliable information. In particular, it requires information on the identity of owners and other stakeholders as well as information on the transactions carried out by entities and other organisational structures. Such information may be kept for tax, regulatory, commercial or other reasons. If such information is not kept or the information is not maintained for a reasonable period of time, a jurisdiction's competent authority[11] may not be able to obtain and provide it when requested. This section of the report describes and assesses Hong Kong's legal and regulatory framework for availability of information. It also assesses the implementation and effectiveness of this framework in practice.

66. Companies formed under Hong Kong law are obliged to register and file annual returns with the Companies Registry that identify the legal owners of the company. Hong Kong companies are also obliged to maintain a register of shareholders in Hong Kong. Public companies limited by shares are permitted to issue share warrants to bearer. While there are no share warrants to bearer in circulation at present, there are currently insufficient mechanisms in place that ensure the availability of information allowing for

11. The term "competent authority" means the person or government authority designated by a jurisdiction as being competent to exchange information pursuant to a double tax convention or tax information exchange agreement.

identification of their owners. The new *Companies Ordinance*, which has been enacted but is not yet in operation, repeals the power of a company to issue share warrants to bearer.

67. Non-Hong Kong companies that have an established place of business in Hong Kong are obliged to register with the Companies Registry and the Business Registration Office. They are not required to disclose ownership information as part of the registration process and tax returns typically do not contain such information. However, non-Hong Kong companies that have established a place of business in Hong Kong need to maintain information about their shareholders to meet their tax obligations. In particular, shareholding information is required to be maintained in order to assess: whether the company is entitled to utilise losses brought forward to set-off against its assessable profits of subsequent years; whether a lender is an associate of a company such that the deduction claim of the respective interest expenses by the company may be denied; whether a non-resident is a closely connected person with the local taxpayer such that the profits of the non-resident is deemed to be taxable profits in Hong Kong and chargeable in the name of the local taxpayer; and whether the Commissioner of Inland Revenue has the power to determine the true market value of assets for the purposes of computing depreciation allowances if the buyer and seller of the assets are related parties.

68. Information is not required to be maintained by nominees where the legal owner of a company acts on behalf of another person as a nominee or under similar arrangement. Financial institutions and attorneys in Hong Kong are, however, subject to AML obligations and obliged to maintain such information if they establish a business relationship with a company.

69. Information is available to Hong Kong's competent authority that identifies the partners in any partnership that has income, deductions or credits for Hong Kong tax purposes, carries on business in Hong Kong, or is a limited partnership formed under Hong Kong law. Such partnerships are obliged to provide an annual partnership return to the IRD identifying all partners in the partnership. In addition, the Companies Registry maintains a public register of all Hong Kong limited partnerships identifying all general and limited partners.

70. For an express trust to be properly constituted in Hong Kong, it is fundamental that there be a settlor and trustee(s). At common law, a trust instrument will contain information on the identity of the settlor and trustee(s). Common law applicable to trusts in Hong Kong requires the maintenance of information that identifies the beneficiaries of express trusts created under the laws of Hong Kong. It is recommended that a statutory obligation be established to maintain information in all cases in relation to settlors, trustees and beneficiaries of trusts with a trustee in Hong Kong.

71. Enforcement provisions are in place to ensure the availability of information in accordance with the international standards.

72. All legal entities and arrangements that carry on a trade, profession, or business in Hong Kong are obliged to maintain a full range of accounting records, including underlying documentation, for a minimum of seven years.

73. Financial institutions operating in Hong Kong are obliged to maintain information on all account-holders and related financial and transactional information.

74. Compliance with all entities' obligations to maintain ownership, accounting and banking information is monitored by the Inland Revenue Department, the Companies Registry and other public authorities, such as the Hong Kong Monetary Authority and the Securities and Futures Commission. Sanctions are set at the appropriate level to ensure compliance with information keeping requirements and such sanctions are regularly enforced in practice.

75. During the period under review (1 July 2009 to 30 June 2012), Hong Kong received a total of 61 requests for information from its treaty partners. Those requests contained 36 inquiries for identity or ownership information, 37 for accounting information and 14 for banking information. The Hong Kong authorities report, and Hong Kong's treaty partners confirm, that information was available when requested. Hong Kong has declined to reply to two requests made by a treaty partner on the basis of absence of a domestic tax interest (more details in parts B and C of this report), since the treaty with the relevant treaty partner did not contain a provision equivalent to article 26(4) of the OECD Model Convention. The information requested in those two cases included contracts and other business records. Hong Kong and that treaty partner have already signed a protocol containing a provision equivalent to article 26(4) of the OECD Model Convention and now Hong Kong is able to provide information in relation to which it has no domestic tax interest to this treaty partner.

A.1. Ownership and identity information

Jurisdictions should ensure that ownership and identity information for all relevant entities and arrangements is available to their competent authorities.

Companies (ToR[12] A.1.1)

76. Hong Kong's *Companies Ordinance* (Cap.32) provides the legal framework for the incorporation and operation of companies in Hong Kong.

12. *Terms of Reference to Monitor and Review Progress Towards Transparency and Exchange of Information.*

The core company provisions of the *Companies Ordinance* (except the winding-up provisions) are administered by the Companies Registry (s. 303). All information held by the Companies Registry on incorporated companies and non-Hong Kong companies having established a place of business in Hong Kong is disclosed in the Companies Registry's registers for public inspection (s. 305). Members of the public are able to obtain company information, including information on the members and directors, online.[13]

Types of companies

77. The *Companies Ordinance* defines "company" as a company formed and registered under the *Companies Ordinance* (s. 2). Any one or more persons may form an incorporated company, with or without limited liability, by complying with the requirements of the *Companies Ordinance* in respect of registration (s. 4). The following types of companies can be incorporated in Hong Kong: public companies limited by shares; private companies limited by shares; guarantee companies without share capital; and unlimited companies with or without share capital (s. 4). Companies limited by shares are companies having the liability of their members limited to the amount, if any, unpaid on the shares respectively held by them (s. 4(2)(a)). Guarantee companies are companies having the liability of their members limited to such amount as the members may respectively undertake to contribute to the assets of the company in the event of it being wound up (s.(4(2)(b)). Unlimited companies are companies not having any limit on the liability of their members (s. 4(2)(c)).

78. Companies can be owned by one or more members, which may be legal or natural persons. Private companies must have at least one director and one company secretary (s. 153A), while public companies must have at least two directors and one company secretary (s. 153). Private companies may have corporate directors. There is no minimum share capital for incorporation in Hong Kong.

79. As at 31 December 2012, there were 1 044 644 locally incorporated companies registered with the Companies Registry. Of those companies, 1 032 863 were private companies limited by shares, 333 were non-listed public companies limited by shares, 205 were listed public companies limited by shares, 11 230 were companies limited by guarantee and 13 were unlimited companies with share capital. There were also 8 848 non-Hong Kong companies registered under the *Companies Ordinance*.

13. Accessible at: www.icris.cr.gov.hk/csci/.

Ownership information on domestic companies

Registration of companies

80. Companies incorporated in Hong Kong are obliged to register with the Companies Registry (s. 14A). The information and documents that must be registered include: the memorandum of association (stating the name, domicile, objects (optional), liability and capital of the company) (s. 5); articles of association (if any) (s. 9); and an incorporation form which contains *inter alia* (s. 14A):

- the name of the company and the address of the company's registered office in Hong Kong;
- a statement as to whether the company is to be limited by shares, limited by guarantee or unlimited (if the company is to be limited by guarantee, the amount that each person who is to be a member undertakes to contribute to its assets if it is wound up);
- the name and address of each founding member of the company and if the company has share capital, the number of shares that each founding member is to take; and
- with respect to each person who on incorporation is to be a director or a company secretary: in the case of an individual, his or her name, residential address and identity card number (if any) otherwise the number and issuing country of any passport held by him or her. In the case of a body corporate, its corporate name and registered or principal office.

81. Upon receipt of a company's application for registration, the Companies Registry issues the company a certificate of incorporation, which is conclusive evidence that all the requirements of the *Companies Ordinance* in respect of registration have been complied with, and that the association is a company authorised to be registered and duly registered (*Companies Ordinance* ss.16, 18).

82. After incorporation, companies are obliged to provide further details of their directors, secretary, registered office address and charges to the Companies Registry for record and public inspection (*Companies Ordinance* s. 158). In addition, all companies are obliged to notify the Companies Registry of any changes to information registered with the Companies Registry within 14 days of the change (s. 158(4)).

83. All companies incorporated in Hong Kong are obliged to file an annual return with the Companies Registry that specifies the names and addresses of its directors and members (*Companies Ordinance* s. 107). The annual return of a private company having share capital must be filed within

42 days after the most recent anniversary of the date of incorporation of the company (s. 109(1)). For a public company, the annual return is to be completed within 42 days after the annual general meeting (s. 109(2)).

84. Hong Kong authorities report that the Companies Registry ensures the accuracy of information maintained in its registries by prosecuting companies which fail to file their annual returns within the prescribed time limit and for other breaches of the *Companies Ordinance*, including failure to update particulars with respect to directors, company secretaries and the registered office or to report the appointment/resignation of directors or company secretaries.

85. Ownership information on current or dissolved Hong Kong incorporated companies is maintained permanently by the Companies Registry (*Companies Ordinance* ss.348D). This includes information on all shareholders as well as changes to shareholding, as disclosed by the companies in their annual returns filed with the Companies Registry. All information on Hong Kong incorporated companies maintained by the Companies Registry is open for public inspection (s. 305).

86. Part XV of the *Securities and Futures Ordinance* contains additional requirements for listed corporations (i.e. publicly traded companies) by requiring certain corporate insiders (e.g. substantial shareholders, directors, chief executives) to give notice to the Hong Kong Stock Exchange on the occurrence of the following events:

- substantial shareholders (i.e. individuals and corporations who are interested in 5% or more of any class of voting shares in a listed corporation) must disclose their interests, and short positions, in voting shares of the listed corporation; and
- directors and chief executives of a listed corporation must disclose their interests, and short positions in any shares in a listed corporation (or any of its associated corporations) and their interests in any debentures of the listed corporation (or any of its associated corporations).

87. These requirements apply to any corporation listed on the Hong Kong Stock Exchange irrespective of whether or not the corporation is incorporated in Hong Kong. The information filed is publicly available and maintained by the Stock Exchange.[14]

14. Information regarding substantial shareholders' interests in a listed company can be found on the internet, e.g. HKEx website. Accessible at: www.hkexnews.hk/di/di.htm.

Registration of companies in practice

88. As at 31 December 2012, the Companies Registry had 291 employees, with 78 of those performing duties relating to registration of companies and monitoring compliance with registration requirements.

89. In February 2011, Hong Kong launched a "one-stop company incorporation and business registration service" under which any person who applies for incorporation of a domestic company under the *Companies Ordinance* is deemed to have made a simultaneous application for business registration. Company incorporation and business registration functions were previously performed separately. Moreover, electronic incorporation of companies and electronic filing of commonly filed company documents have also been implemented since March 2011. In order to incorporate a company electronically, one of the founders must first register as a user of the Companies Registry's e-Registry. Identity information of this founder must be provided as part of the registration process and is verified by the Companies Registry before documents can be signed and submitted via the e-Registry. The founder who signs the incorporation form has to certify in that form that the particulars contained therein are accurate. It is also an offence to furnish false information in any return or other document required by the Companies Ordinance (s. 349).

90. The Companies Registry maintains a computerised database containing relevant information on companies, including the name and address of companies, particulars of directors, secretaries and authorised representatives as well as each company's share capital. The Companies Registry's database is open for public inspection. The annual returns filed by companies are kept permanently and are also open for public inspection. The IRD may inspect and retrieve information from the Companies Registry's database and uses it to reply to most requests concerning ownership information on Hong Kong companies.

91. The Companies Registry has a system that monitors the filing of annual returns. The system automatically detects companies which fail to file annual returns by the due date. In order to encourage companies to file annual returns before any prosecution action is initiated, the Companies Registry has introduced a "notice to file" scheme. Companies that are in default of their obligations receive a notice and are given a period of 28 days from the date of the notice to rectify the default. For annual returns required to be filed in 2012, 87.97% of Hong Kong companies and 94.62% of non-Hong Kong companies complied with their filing obligations.

92. Subsequent actions against companies in default are taken, including sending reminders, making enquiries, initiating prosecution actions and striking off actions. These follow up actions may, depending on the time of default in the year and circumstances of the case, not necessarily take place

in the same year but the following year(s). Summonses are issued for prosecution if annual returns remain outstanding after the expiry of the 28-day grace period. In 2012, 6 209 Hong Kong companies (0.59% of the total Hong Kong Companies registered with the Companies Registry) and 86 non-Hong Kong companies (0.97% of the total Hong Kong companies registered with the Companies Registry) were prosecuted by the Registrar for non-compliance with their obligation to file annual returns. The Companies Registry strikes off defunct companies from the register (i.e. companies that are not carrying on business or in operation). The Hong Kong authorities informed that, subject to the facts and circumstances of the individual case, normally a company is considered as defunct if it is in continuous default of filing annual returns for three years. Companies are considered to be defunct if they continuously fail to file annual returns. In 2012 approximately 28 000 companies were struck off (which represents 2.68% of the total Hong Kong companies registered with the Companies Registry).

Company membership registries

93. The *Companies Ordinance* obliges every company incorporated in Hong Kong to maintain a register of members (s. 95). The register must include the following information:

- the names and addresses of the members, the shares or stock held by each member, the distinguishing number of each share if it has a number, and the amount paid on the shares;
- the date at which each person was entered on the register; and
- the date at which any person ceased to be a member.

94. The register of members must be kept at the registered office of the company and in a legible form which does not restrict its availability for public inspection (*Companies Ordinance* s. 95(2)). A company can keep its register of members at a location within Hong Kong other than its registered office location provided the company sends notice to the Companies Registry of the place where its register of members is kept (s. 95(3)). All entries in the register of members relating to persons who cease to be members must be retained for 30 years (s. 95(1)).

95. Pursuant to the Companies Ordinance, the register of members must be open for public inspection (s. 98(1)). The Companies Registry conducts investigations upon receipt of a complaint that a company has failed to make its register of members available for inspection. The Hong Kong authorities report that, in the years 2010-12, there were four cases of complaint. If a company fails to keep a register of its members as required by the Companies Ordinance, the company and its officers are liable for prosecution. During

the period under review, no prosecutions were launched in connection to a company and/or its officers' failure to keep a register of members. Moreover, as described above, the Companies Registry closely monitors the filing of annual returns (which includes information on shareholders) and takes enforcement action where there is non-compliance.

Tax law

96. The IRD administers the *Business Registration Ordinance* (Cap.310) which governs the tax registration of businesses in Hong Kong. Business registration, unlike registration under the *Companies Ordinance*, does not regulate business activities in Hong Kong (neither is it a licence to trade). Its main objectives are to provide the IRD with information on businesses so that tax files can be opened and updated in a timely manner and to enable the public to obtain information on businesses with which they are dealing.

97. The *Business Registration Ordinance* requires "every person commencing to carry on any business or carrying on any business" to apply for business registration with the Commissioner of Inland Revenue, and to display a valid business registration certificate at the place of business (ss.5, 12). In particular, the following businesses are required to be registered:

- any form of trade, commerce, craftsmanship, profession, calling or other activity carried on for the purpose of gain;
- any club that provides facilities, services and exclusive club premises to its members for social intercourse or recreation;
- every company incorporated in Hong Kong in accordance with the *Companies Ordinance* or non-Hong Kong company that has established a place of business in Hong Kong, regardless of whether it is actually carrying on any business in Hong Kong; and
- every non-Hong Kong company that has a representative or liaison office in Hong Kong, or has let out its property situated in Hong Kong, regardless of whether it has established a place of business in Hong Kong.[15]

98. The application for business registration (Form 1(b)) for a Hong Kong incorporated company must be completed by a director, manager or the secretary of the company and must set forth: the full registered name of the company; the address of the registered office in Hong Kong and place of business; the date of incorporation; and a copy of the certificate of incorporation.

15. Inland Revenue Department Guidelines, "Business Required to be Registered and Application for Business Registration". Accessible at: www.ird.gov.hk/eng/tax/bre_abr.htm.

In February 2011, upon the coming into operation of the *Business Registration (Amendment) Ordinance 2010*, members of the public must apply for company incorporation and business registration simultaneously. Since then, the information previously reported in Form 1(b) is included in the application form for company incorporation.

99. The *Inland Revenue Ordinance* s. 51(1) provides that all companies chargeable to profits tax are required to furnish a completed tax return within a reasonable time, normally one month. If the company is chargeable to profits tax for any year of assessment and has not received a tax return from the IRD, it is required to inform the Commissioner of Inland Revenue in writing that it is so chargeable within four months after the end of the basis period for the year of assessment concerned (s. 51(2)). Companies that are not carrying on a trade, profession or business in Hong Kong and do not have any income sourced in Hong Kong are not required file tax returns, unless they have been prompted to do so by the IRD. The IRD reports that, from time to time, it issues tax returns to those companies with no profits chargeable to tax to review their tax positions. The Hong Kong authorities report that the review process is on-going. Companies' tax affairs are reviewed at least once every four years. Specific cases (e.g. loss making companies) are subject to more frequent reviews. The review cycle covers all companies with no profits chargeable to tax, except those companies which have reported the cessation of business. In cases where a company that has reported that it has ceased business, recommences business in future, that company is obliged to notify the IRD of its chargeability to tax and is subject to penalties if it fails to do so. The IRD also cross checks information (e.g. if a company that has reported the cessation of business hires employees, this would trigger further investigation by the IRD).

100. Under s. 2(1A) of the *Business Registration Ordinance*, a company which is incorporated in Hong Kong or a non-Hong Kong company which is liable for Registration in Hong Kong under the Companies Ordinance is deemed to be a person carrying on a business and is liable for registration under the *Business Registration Ordinance*. Upon the coming into operation of the *Business Registration (Amendment) Ordinance 2010*, simultaneous application for company incorporation and business registration is mandatory and profits tax files are opened instantly for all companies registered with the Companies Registry. Accordingly, the requirements and obligations imposed under the *Inland Revenue Ordinance* apply to all companies, even though some of them may not have profits chargeable to tax.

Business Registration in practice

101. In practice, since February 2011, when the *Business Registration (Amendment) Ordinance 2010* took effect, Hong Kong has established a "one-stop service" covering both company incorporation and business registration. The Hong Kong authorities report that the Companies Registry transmits particulars of successfully registered companies to the IRD so that the IRD can keep a database of all companies and businesses registered under the *Business Registration Ordinance.*

102. The IRD has a programme of on-site inspections and has identified cases of failure to register a business. It has an active programme to monitor compliance with legal requirements and has instituted prosecutions where non-compliance was detected. Approximately 15 000 to 20 000 on-site visits were conducted each year from 2009 to 2012. The Hong Kong authorities report that, since the implementation of the "one-stop service", the IRD and the Companies Registry supplement one another and the IRD's work is focused on the registration of sole proprietorships and partnerships as well as enforcing other provisions of the *Business Registration Ordinance*. Cases where unregistered businesses were identified have led to prosecutions. Approximately 2 500-4 000 prosecutions took place each year from 2009 to 2012 in connection with the failure to register a business in Hong Kong.

Ownership information on foreign companies

Registration of foreign companies

103. A non-Hong Kong company which is a body corporate and has established a place of business in Hong Kong is required to apply for registration within one month of the establishment of the place of business in Hong Kong (*Companies Ordinance* s. 333). The company is also required to register with the Business Registration Office.

104. A "place of business" is defined under the *Companies Ordinance* to include a share transfer or share registration office (s. 341) but, according to the 24th Schedule to the ordinance, does not include a local representative office established or maintained with the approval of the Hong Kong Monetary Authority (HKMA) under the *Banking Ordinance* (s. 46). It is necessary to consider the office's main activities in the light of the company's paramount and subsidiary objects and see whether such activities create legal obligations.[16] If they do, the office must register under the *Companies Ordinance*.

16. *Elscint (Asia Pacific) Ltd v. Commercial Bank of Korea Ltd* [1994] HKLY 182; *Murdock v. Dresser-Rand Services SARL* [2002] HKEC 52.

105. Non-Hong Kong companies are required to provide the Companies Registry with the following information (*Companies Ordinance* s. 333):

- the name and place of incorporation of the company;
- copies of the company's constitution;
- lists of directors (names and addresses), company secretary and authorised representative(s) in Hong Kong who can accept service of process on the company's behalf; and
- certificate of incorporation issued in the home jurisdiction and accounts (where the non-Hong Kong company is required by the law of its place of incorporation or any regulator to prepare and file such accounts).

106. Upon receipt of a non-Hong Kong company's application for registration, the Companies Registry retains the registered documents, enters the name of the company on the register of non-Hong Kong companies, and issues a registration certificate to the company (s. 333AA).

107. Details of any changes in the above information must be filed with the Companies Registry within one month of the change (ss.333, 333A, 333B, 335, 336). In addition, an annual return containing the above information must also be submitted within 42 days after the anniversary date of registration of the company in Hong Kong (s. 334).

108. The *Companies Ordinance* does not require non-Hong Kong companies to keep a register of members in Hong Kong. It does, however, provide that if, by virtue of law in any place outside Hong Kong, non-Hong Kong companies have the power to keep in Hong Kong branch registers of their members resident in Hong Kong, the Chief Executive in Council may order every such branch register to be kept in Hong Kong (s. 106). If such order is made, the branch register may only contain identity information on the non-Hong Kong company's resident members.

109. All information held by the Companies Registry on non-Hong Kong companies with a place of business in Hong Kong is disclosed in the Companies Registry's registers for public inspection.

110. Non-Hong Kong companies listed and traded in Hong Kong are obliged to maintain, or make arrangement to maintain, a register of shareholders, or at least a branch register of members in Hong Kong. The registers must be made available for inspection by the public and shareholders under the Listing Rules (see above for disclosure requirements).

Registration of foreign companies in practice

111. Since February 2011, the one-stop service also covers the registration of non-Hong Kong companies (except when the company has already obtained a business registration certificate prior to the application for registration as a non-Hong Kong company under the *Companies Ordinance*). The one-stop service covers registration with both the Companies Registry and the Business Registration Office. As at 31 December 2012, there were 8 848 non-Hong Kong companies registered in Hong Kong.

112. Non-Hong Kong companies that fail to file annual returns with the Companies Registry within 42 days after the anniversary of the date of registration in Hong Kong are also automatically selected by the Registry's system to receive a notice to file. The companies are given a period of 28 days from the date of the notice to rectify the default. The Hong Kong authorities reported that notices to file are to all non-Hong Kong companies in default. Subsequent actions against companies in default are taken, including sending reminders, making enquiries, initiating prosecution actions and striking off actions. These follow up actions may, depending on the time of default in the year and circumstances of the case, not necessarily take place in the same year but the following year(s). Summonses are issued for prosecution if annual returns remain outstanding after the 28-day grace period expires. The compliance rate of non-Hong Kong companies with their obligation to file annual returns is very high: 94.62% of the total registered non-Hong Kong companies complied with their filing obligations in a timely manner in 2012. In the same year, 86 non-Hong Kong companies were summoned for non-compliance with their obligation to file annual returns to the Companies Registry.

Tax law

113. Non-Hong Kong companies commencing to carry on any business in Hong Kong are obliged to apply for business registration with the Commissioner of Inland Revenue, and to display a valid business registration certificate at the place of business (*Business Registration Ordinance* ss.5, 12). The application for business registration (Form 1(b)) for a non-Hong Kong company must be completed by a director, manager or the secretary of the company and must set forth:

- the full registered name of the company and place of incorporation;
- the name and address of person(s) resident in Hong Kong whose particulars have been delivered to the Companies Registry;
- the date of registration under the *Companies Ordinance;* a copy of the certificate of registration of a non-Hong Kong company or a copy of the certificate of incorporation (or its equivalent) issued by the relevant government authority of its place of incorporation; and

- the business name (if any), nature of business activities, address of the place of business and date of commencement of business in Hong Kong.

114. Obligations on domestic companies apply equally to non-Hong Kong companies. The *Inland Revenue Ordinance* provides that all companies are required to furnish within a reasonable time, normally one month, any tax return issued by the IRD (s. 51(1)). If a company is chargeable to profits tax for any year of assessment and has not received a tax return it is required to inform the IRD in writing that the company is so chargeable, within 4 months after the end of the basis period for the year of assessment concerned (s. 51(2)). There is no difference in the return filing requirement based on whether a company is owned by residents or non-residents.

115. Under s. 2(1A) of the *Business Registration Ordinance*, a non-Hong Kong company which is registered in Hong Kong is deemed to be a person carrying on a business and is liable for registration under the *Business Registration Ordinance*. Upon the coming into operation of the *Business Registration (Amendment) Ordinance 2010*, simultaneous application for company incorporation and business registration is mandatory and profits tax files are opened instantly for all companies registered with the Companies Registry. Accordingly, the requirements and obligations imposed under the *Inland Revenue Ordinance* apply to all companies regardless of whether they have profits chargeable to tax in Hong Kong.

116. Non-Hong Kong companies are not required to set out details of their owners in the profits tax return. However, there is a field in the return (BIR 51 item 7.6.1) whereby private companies, whether local or foreign, are required to specify whether there is any change in shareholders during the basis period. Such ownership information may be requested by the tax authorities in the course of examining taxpayers' profits tax returns. There are various provisions in the *Inland Revenue Ordinance* whereby ownership information is relevant in ascertaining a taxpayer's tax liabilities. These include: (a) s. 61B – whether the company is entitled to utilise losses brought forward to set-off against its assessable profits of subsequent years; (b) s. 16(2) – whether the lender is an associate of a company such that the deduction claim of the respective interest expenses by the company may be denied; (c) s. 20 – whether a non-resident is a closely connected person with the local taxpayer such that the profits of the non-resident is deemed to be taxable profits in Hong Kong and chargeable in the name of the local taxpayer; and (d) s. 38B – where the Commissioner of Inland Revenue has the power to determine the true market value of assets for the purposes of computing depreciation allowances if the buyer and seller of the assets are related parties. Accordingly, companies, whether local or foreign, are obliged to maintain ownership information in order to meet their tax obligations.

Tax obligations of foreign companies in practice

117. A non-Hong Kong company carrying on a business in Hong Kong is subject to the same reporting requirements as a Hong Kong company. The IRD does not keep separate statistics on the compliance by non-Hong Kong companies with their tax filing obligations. The IRD report that information on the ownership of non-Hong Kong companies was available when requested for domestic purposes. To date, Hong Kong has not received any EOI requests concerning the ownership of non-Hong Kong companies.

Ownership information held by directors and officers

118. Directors and officers of Hong Kong companies are not statutorily required to maintain ownership information in respect of the company. These requirements lie on the company. The Hong Kong authorities advise that the requirement to maintain information on a company's shareholders rests on the company and every officer of it, as both the company and its officers are subject to sanctions if they are in default (s. 95 (4)). Officers are defined in the Companies Ordinance as a director, manager or secretary (s. 2).

119. The *Companies Ordinance* provides that companies are obliged to have a company secretary (s. 154). If the company secretary is an individual he or she must be a Hong Kong resident and if a body corporate it must have its registered office or a place of business in Hong Kong (s. 154(2)). Public companies and private companies which are members of a group of which a listed company is a member are not permitted to have corporate directors (s. 154A). While directors and company secretaries are not directly obliged to maintain information on the owners of their companies, they will have access to the company's register of members because, as set out above, the *Companies Ordinance* requires every company incorporated in Hong Kong to keep and maintain a register of members.

Ownership information held by service providers

120. Hong Kong's AML regime is derived from the *Anti-Money Laundering and Counter-Terrorist Financing (Financial Institutions) Ordinance* (Cap.615) (*AMLO*), the *Drug Trafficking (Recovery of Proceeds) Ordinance* (Cap.405) (DTROP), the *Organized and Serious Crimes Ordinance* (Cap.455) (OSCO) and the *United Nations (Anti-Terrorism Measures) Ordinance* (Cap.575) *(UNATMO)*. The *DTROP*, the *OSCO* and the *UNATMO* require reporting of suspicious transactions regarding money laundering or terrorist financing and apply to all persons and entities in Hong Kong, including financial institutions, without exception. The wider responsibilities of financial institutions in respect of customer due diligence (CDD), record-keeping, etc, which are preventative measures for money laundering, are set out in the *AMLO*.

121. The *AMLO* was enacted on 29 June 2011, and entered into force on 1 April 2012. Prior to the enactment of the *AMLO*, mandatory AML guidelines issued by the relevant authorities under their respective governing ordinances stipulated CDD and record-keeping requirements. While these guidelines did not have the force of law, the regulators could enforce them using a range of supervisory powers or administrative measures.

122. The *AMLO* codified CDD and record-keeping requirements in a single piece of legislation applicable to all specified financial sectors. It also provides relevant sanctions for failure to comply and enforcement powers for regulatory authorities. The law imposes obligations on a wide range of financial institutions, including banks, corporations licensed by the Securities and Futures Commission, authorised insurers, insurance agents and brokers and licensed money service operators.

123. Pursuant to the *AMLO*, financial institutions must identify and verify the identity of their customers and identify and take reasonable measures to verify the identity of the customer's beneficial owner(s) before establishing a business relationship (Schedule 2, ss.2 and 3). Financial institutions must also keep records relevant to their customer's and beneficial owner's identity as well as transaction records for at least six years following the completion of the transaction, or the end of business (as the case may be) (Schedule 2, s.20). As part of the obligation to perform reasonable measures to verify the identity of the beneficial owners of a corporate customer, financial institutions must verify the identity of any individual that holds or controls, directly or indirectly, including through a trust or bearer share holding, at least a 25% interest in the corporate customer (i.e. 25% of the entity's share capital or 25% of the voting rights at general meetings) (Schedule 2, s.2(2)). In high-risk cases, the CDD obligations are stricter and financial institutions must take reasonable measures to verify the identity of any individuals holding at least a 10% interest (Schedule 2, ss.1, 2 and 15). If the corporate customer is acting on behalf of another person, the financial institutions must identify that other person, irrespective of whether the case is of high risk or not (Schedule 2, ss.1 and 2). The *AMLO* adopts a risk-based approach concerning the monitoring of existing customer relationships.

124. Uniform guidance relating to the operation of the above-mentioned provisions of Schedule 2 of the *AMLO* is provided in the AML/CFT guidelines issued by the Securities and Futures Commission (SFC)[17], the Hong

17. In addition, under the Code of Conduct for SFC's licensed or registered persons, which was gazetted under the *Securities and Futures Ordinance*, licensed corporations have the duty to find out whether a client is acting as principal or agent (paragraph 5.4 and client identity guidance note in Schedule 2 applicable to transactions involving securities or futures contracts that are listed or traded on a recognised stock market or a recognised futures market or a derivative, including

Kong Monetary Authority, Office of the Commissioner of Insurance and the Customs and Excise Department for their respective sectors.

125. In addition to financial institutions, certain non-financial professionals are subject to AML/CFT guidelines or best practices issued by their respective professional bodies. The Law Society of Hong Kong issued a mandatory practice direction on AML/Counter-Terrorist Financing in December 2007 which took effect from 1 July 2008 (Guide to Professional Conduct Vol. 2, Chapter 24, Practice Directions). Under its mandatory provisions, lawyers, including foreign lawyers practising in Hong Kong, are obliged to identify and verify the identities of their clients and their beneficial owners before establishing a business relationship or when carrying out occasional transactions and to keep records relevant to their clients' identity as well as transaction records (paras. 18-26). Files, including CDD records, must be kept for a period of: 15 years for conveyancing matters; seven years for tenancy matters; seven years for other matters (except criminal cases); and three years from expiration of any appeal period for criminal matters (para. 6). The practice direction is a set of mandatory guidelines which carry sanctions. Practitioners who fail to comply with the requirements are liable to disciplinary action by the Law Society of Hong Kong ranging from a fine to revoking or suspending a solicitor's licence to practise in Hong Kong. The Law Society of Hong Kong is not aware of any breaches so far and, hence, has not applied any sanctions in connection with the mandatory practice direction on AML/CFT to date.

126. As regards other professional service providers in Hong Kong (e.g. company secretaries, trustees who are not lawyers and accountants), there are no mandatory obligations to conduct CDD, though a number of professional codes of ethics or regulatory and self-regulatory standards provide non-mandatory CDD guidance.[18] Moreover, these professional service providers have not yet implemented formal structures to monitor their members' compliance with the AML/CFT guidelines and best practices. The Hong Kong authorities report, however, that they are taking progressive steps to extend CDD and record-keeping obligations to all relevant Designated Non-Financial Businesses

---

an over-the-counter derivative, written over such securities or futures contracts). If the client is acting as an agent, the licensed institution must be satisfied on reasonable grounds of the identity, address and contact details of the principal.

18. Hong Kong's Narcotics Division of the Security Bureau published the Practical Guide on Anti-Money Laundering & Counter-Terrorist Financing in June 2009. The Hong Kong Institute of Certified Public Accountants issued an advisory Legal Bulletin in July 2006. The Estate Agents Authority has issued practice circulars on AML/Counter-Terrorist Financing since 2004. The Hong Kong Institute of Chartered Secretaries promulgated advisory guidelines for its members in May 2008 and issued a CDD checklist in 2010.

and Professions, which cover trust and company service providers, in line with the updated FATF recommendations. These steps include issuing guidance, conducting outreach and capacity building seminars, publishing a training kit and examining alternatives to improve the current legal framework.

Ownership information held by nominees

127. The *Terms of Reference* requires that jurisdictions ensure that information is available to their competent authorities that identify the owners of companies and any bodies corporate. Owners include legal owners, and, in any case where a legal owner acts on behalf of another person as a nominee or under a similar arrangement, that other person, as well as persons in an ownership chain, to the extent that it is held by the jurisdiction's authorities or is within the possession or control of persons within the jurisdiction's territorial jurisdiction.

128. Currently nominees are not explicitly required to know the ultimate beneficial owner of shares being held on behalf of another person. Nominees should know who they are acting for but there is no requirement for them to retain identity information on the persons for whom they act as legal owner. Additionally, there is no requirement in the *Companies Ordinance* for companies to indicate whether shares are held beneficially or not. The *Companies Ordinance* expressly provides that no notice of any trust, expressed, implied, or constructive, shall be entered on the register, or be receivable by the Companies Registry (s. 101). Hong Kong authorities report that in practice nominee contracts are in writing and maintained by nominee shareholders even though there is no legal requirement for such contracts to be in writing.

129. The Hong Kong authorities also report that those agreements, commonly referred to as a "declaration of trust", are in many instances delivered to the stamp office of the IRD for adjudication. The Hong Kong authorities report that declarations of trust in respect of a Hong Kong stock which involve the transfer of beneficial interest in the underlying stock is a chargeable instrument under the *Stamp Duty Ordinance* (Cap.117 head 2(3) of Schedule 1) and must be submitted to the IRD for stamping. In practice, the Hong Kong authorities report that declarations of trust which do not involve change of beneficial interest in the underlying stock are also submitted to the IRD for adjudication.

130. There are certain requirements for identification of persons on whose behalf nominees act under the AML framework. Hong Kong's mandatory AML obligations for financial institutions (namely banks, securities firms and insurance institutions) require them to identify the beneficial owners of a corporation, including those who directly or indirectly, own or control a certain percentage of the shares or the voting right of the corporation and to verify their identity. The identification and verification of the identity of beneficial

owners are subject to different thresholds in Hong Kong. The threshold applicable to the identification requirement is 10%. The threshold applicable to the verification requirement is 25%, except in high risk cases[19], where the applicable threshold is 10% (AMLO, Schedule 2, s. 2). Under the *mandatory practice direction*, lawyers are required to, for a corporate client, identify the person purporting to give instructions on behalf of the client and to identify and understand the beneficial ownership and control structure of the client. The Hong Kong Institute of Certified Public Accountants specified in its advisory guidelines that when an accountant is acting or arranging for another person to act as a nominee shareholder, the accountant should perform CDD to identify the beneficial owner and to understand the ownership and control structure of the customer. The Hong Kong Institute of Chartered Secretaries, a professional body, issued advisory guidelines reminding company secretaries to be suspicious of a customer who undertakes a transaction on behalf of another person without sufficient identification of his or her nominee capacity and that they should make further enquiries as to the underlying principals. The guidelines of the professional bodies, being advisory in nature, do not have the force of law. It is recommended, however, that an obligation should be imposed that all nominees maintain relevant ownership information where they act as the legal owners on behalf of any other person.

131. As regards listed corporations, the *Securities and Futures Ordinance* requires substantial shareholders (i.e. individuals and corporations who are interested in 5% or more of any class of voting shares in a listed corporation) as well as directors and chief executives to disclose their interests in shares of the listed corporation, even if the shares are held for them by another person such as a stockbroker, custodian, trustee or nominee. It also allows a listed corporation to make enquiries to establish who owns its shares (s. 329).[20] A listed corporation may also investigate the ownership of equity derivatives where the underlying shares of the equity derivatives are shares in the listed corporation concerned.

132. Pursuant to the *Inland Revenue Ordinance,* Hong Kong's IRD has the power to require a nominee to identify the person on whose behalf securities are held (s. 51(4)). If a person is unwilling to disclose the identity of the person for whom they act as legal owner they can be subject to penalties for failing to comply with the notice (see part B.1 of this report).

19. Concerning "high-risk", the AML Ordinance refers to "a situation specified by the relevant authority in a notice in writing given to the financial institution and in any other situation that by its nature may present a high risk of money laundering or terrorist financing" (AMLO, Schedule 2, s. 15).

20. The powers are not limited to establishing the identities of the substantial shareholders (i.e. persons holding 5% or more of the shares) but extend to any person that has, or had, an interest or a short position in its shares.

Bearer shares *(ToR A.1.2)*

133. Public companies limited by shares are permitted, if so authorised by their articles of incorporation, to issue share warrants to bearer, i.e. a warrant stating that the bearer of the warrant is entitled to the shares specified in it (*Companies Ordinance* s. 73). The issuance of share warrants to bearer is required to be reflected in a company's register of members, which is available for public inspection (s. 97). In the event of a transfer of share warrants to bearer, the name of the new shareholder is entered in the share register if he or his lawful representative gives the company notice of the change of ownership and proves his right (s. 97(2)).

134. Hong Kong authorities report that there are no share warrants to bearer in circulation. As at 31 December 2012, only 538 public companies limited by shares are allowed to issue share warrants to bearer. Further, Hong Kong's Stock Exchange reports that it has not encountered any Hong Kong incorporated issuers (205 in number) issuing share warrants to bearer. The issuance of share warrants to bearer by a private company is prohibited by the restriction on the transfer of shares under the *Companies Ordinance* s. 29.[21] As a result, only 333 unlisted public companies limited by shares may issue share warrants to bearer. Further, and based on a recent examination of records maintained by the Companies Registry with respect to these companies, Hong Kong authorities report that there are currently no share warrants to bearer issued by these companies. The new Companies Ordinance, which has been enacted but is not yet in operation, repeals the power of a company to issue share warrants to bearer (see more details later in this section).

135. As mentioned in section A.1.1 above, financial institutions and lawyers are obliged to conduct CDD on their customers, including identification of their beneficial owners. Additionally, financial institutions are required to exercise special care in dealing with public companies limited by shares which have a significant proportion of capital in the form of share warrants to bearer (paragraph 4.14 of the AML guidelines issued by relevant authorities setting out the CDD requirements for bearer shares).

136. Moreover, pursuant to the *Stamp Duty Ordinance* (Cap.117), the issuance of share warrants to bearer is chargeable with stamp duty (Head 3 of the First Schedule). The Hong Kong authorities advised that stamping must take place before share warrants to bearer are issued. Given the mandatory stamping requirement under the *Stamp Duty Ordinance*, the Hong Kong authorities are able to check the records of the IRD to determine if any share warrants to

21. The *Companies Ordinance* defines "private company" as a company which by its articles: restricts the right to transfer its shares; limits the number of its members to 50; and prohibits any invitation to the public to subscribe for any shares or debentures of the company (s. 29).

bearer have been issued. Similarly, the IRD is able to monitor the issuance of share warrants to bearer in the future, as such share warrants would attract stamp duty. The Hong Kong authorities confirmed that the IRD maintains records of the details of the share warrants presented for stamping, with paper files opened to keep all the documents submitted and the stamping records for each share warrants stamping application, and, thus, the IRD would be able to monitor the issuance of such warrants by checking the above mentioned records and files. The IRD confirmed that, according to their records, no share warrants to bearer have been stamped since the last verification was conducted at the time of Hong Kong's Phase 1 review. Failure to stamp a share warrant has the following consequences: *(i)* the share warrant cannot be admitted as evidence in court until it is stamped (s. 15(1)); *(ii)* a company that changes the register of members before it is stamped is liable to a penalty on conviction, at level two (equivalent to HKD 5 000 or EUR 494) (*Stamp Duty Ordinance* s. 15(2) and *Companies Ordinance* s. 97)); *(iii)* there is a penalty for late stamping of an amount equivalent to 10 times the amount of the stamp duty chargeable on the share warrant (s. 5(5)).

137. The *new Companies Ordinance,* passed by Hong Kong's Legislative Council in July 2012, will come into operation on a day to be appointed by the Secretary for Financial Services and the Treasury by notice published in the Gazette. It is expected that the new *Companies Ordinance* will come into operation in the first quarter of 2014. The law repeals a company's power to issue share warrants to bearer (s. 139(1)), whilst imposing no obligation on the holders of any share warrants to bearer issued prior to the effective date of the *new Companies Ordinance* to surrender their share warrant for cancellation. While there is a possibility that information on such holders would remain undisclosed, it is noted that in practice there are mechanisms to check whether a bearer share warrant has been issued in Hong Kong and the number of companies that currently have this capacity is limited. The Hong Kong authorities also report, as mentioned above, that currently there are no share warrants to bearer in circulation. During the three year period under review, no concerns have been raised by Hong Kong's EOI partners in relation to bearer share warrants issued by companies formed under Hong Kong law.

Conclusion and practice

138. Companies formed under Hong Kong law are obliged to register and file annual returns with the Companies Registry that identify the legal owners of the company. Hong Kong companies are also obliged to maintain a register of shareholders in Hong Kong. Public companies limited by shares are permitted to issue share warrants to bearer. While there are no share warrants to bearer in circulation at present, there are currently insufficient mechanisms in place that ensure the availability of information allowing for identification of their owners.

139. In practice, ownership information is filed with the Companies Registry and is stored in a database maintained by it. Companies are also statutorily required to keep registers of members. Both the Companies Registry's database and the register of members kept by companies are open for public inspection. The IRD may inspect and retrieve information from the Companies Registry's database and uses it to reply to most requests concerning ownership information on Hong Kong companies. The IRD can also request ownership information directly from the company concerned.

140. Non-Hong Kong companies that have an established place of business in Hong Kong are obliged to register with the Companies Registry and the Business Registration Office. They are not required to disclose ownership information as part of the registration process and tax returns typically do not contain such information. However, non-Hong Kong companies that have established a place of business in Hong Kong need to maintain information about their shareholders to meet their tax obligations.

141. Information is not required to be maintained by nominees where the legal owner of a company acts on behalf of another person as a nominee or under similar arrangement. Financial institutions and attorneys in Hong Kong are, however, subject to AML obligations and obliged to maintain such information if they establish a business relationship with a company.

142. The Hong Kong authorities maintain statistics of incoming requests for information on the identity or ownership of legal entities (including companies, partnerships, etc.). During the period under review, 34 EOI requests concerning identity or ownership information of companies were received and answered by the Hong Kong authorities. The comments provided by Hong Kong's EOI partners confirmed that ownership information of companies was one of the categories of information requested. They have also reported that information was provided in a timely manner. During the three year period under review, no issues have been raised in relation to bearer share warrants by Hong Kong's EOI partners.

Partnerships (ToR A.1.3)

143. Hong Kong law provides for the creation of two types of partnerships: general partnerships governed by the *Partnership Ordinance* (Cap.38); and limited partnerships governed by the *Limited Partnerships Ordinance* (Cap.37). As at 31 December 2012, there were approximately 31 000 partnerships registered with the Business Registration Office and 163 limited partnerships registered with the Companies Registry.

144. Pursuant to the *Limited Partnerships Ordinance* s.3, a limited partnership must consist of one or more general partners, who have unlimited liability and one or more limited partners with limited liability. A limited

partner cannot take part in the management of the partnership business and cannot have power to bind the firm (s. 5). A partnership is deemed to be a general partnership unless one or more partners are registered as limited partners under the *Limited Partnerships Ordinance* (s. 4). The *Limited Partnerships Ordinance* applies to partnerships carrying on business in Hong Kong (s. 2).

145. The *Partnership Ordinance* s. 3 defines "partnership" as the relation which subsists between persons carrying on a business in common with a view of profit. As such, all partnerships carrying on business in Hong Kong should be chargeable to profits tax under the *Inland Revenue Ordinance* (s. 14) and are subject to the relevant accounting and documentation requirements under the *Ordinance*.

Ownership information held by government authorities

Registration of partnerships

146. The *Business Registration Ordinance* requires every person who carries on a business in Hong Kong to apply for business registration within one month from the date of commencement of the business, and to display a valid Business Registration Certificate at the place of business. Regardless of the types of partnerships or partners (limited or unlimited), the particulars of a partnership furnished in its application for business registration are recorded and maintained permanently by the Business Registration Office of the IRD.

147. Upon registration, every business including partnerships is assigned a unique business registration number. The IRD will record the information provided in the applications for registration and the notifications of change on the Business Register. The public can obtain extracts of the information on the Business Register upon payment of a fee. The application for business registration (Form 1(c)) for general and limited partnerships must set forth:

- the business name and address;
- the nature of business and date of commencement (and cessation, if any); and
- the name, the Hong Kong Identity Card number or passport number, and residential address of all the partners.

148. Business registration must be renewed annually, unless the business applies for a three-year Business Registration Certificate. Notifications of any change in the particulars set out in the form of application for registration or cessation of business must be submitted to the Business Registration Office within one month of such change or cessation (s. 8). Ownership details set out in the application form for business registration are kept on a permanent

basis, and the records for the subsequent notifications of change of partners is kept for 11 years (s. 8).

149. In addition, every limited partnership must be registered with the Companies Registry in accordance with the provisions of the *Limited Partnership Ordinance*, or in default thereof will be deemed to be a general partnership and every limited partner is deemed to be a general partner (s. 4). The following particulars are required to be given to the Companies Registry in the form of a statement for registration of a limited partnership (s. 7):

- the firm's name and its principal place of business;
- the general nature of the business;
- the full name of each of the partners;
- the term, if any, for which the partnership is entered into, and the date of its commencement;
- a statement that the partnership is limited, and the description of every limited partner as such; and
- the sum contributed by each limited partner, and whether paid in cash or how otherwise.

150. If any change occurs to the above particulars during the continuance of a limited partnership, a statement specifying the nature of the change must be given to the Companies Registry within 7 days (*Limited Partnership Ordinance* s. 8). The *Limited Partnership Ordinance* requires the Companies Registry to keep a register and an index of all limited partnerships and imaged records of all statements registered under the ordinance (s. 13). The register and imaged records are retained permanently by the Companies Registry even after the dissolution of the partnership.

151. The Companies Registry maintains an index of limited partnerships. The statements registered under the *Limited Partnership Ordinance* in respect of each limited partnership are available for public inspection. The particulars reported in the statements include, among others, the full name of each of the partners of the limited partnership. Moreover, the IRD maintains a computerised database containing relevant information on partnerships including the name of the partners of both general and limited partnerships.

152. According to the Companies Registry's records, the 163 existing limited partnerships are engaged in investment, stockbrokerage, financial services and related businesses (23.1%), shipping businesses (21.9%), video games and related business (12.4%), restaurants and related businesses (7.1%), other businesses (35.5%).

153. The Companies Registry investigates when a complaint is filed against the limited partnership (e.g. by a third party such as a partner or former partner). The Companies Registry reports that in the period under review it has not received any complaints concerning compliance by limited partnerships with their filing obligations under the *Limited Partnership Ordinance.* Verification of partnerships' tax filing obligations is carried out by the IRD (please see section below).

Tax law

154. The *Inland Revenue Ordinance* provides that all partnerships are required to furnish within a reasonable time, normally one month, a completed tax return (ss.22 and 51(1)). The profits or losses of partnerships in Hong Kong are assessed in one sum and tax is charged in the partnership's name (s.22). The tax may be recoverable from the assets of the partnership or the partners directly even if the partnership has dissolved (s.22). Partners, being individuals, may elect for Personal Assessment, a method of tax computation, to have their share of profits or losses generated by the partnership taxed in their own name instead of in name of the partnership (s.41). The partners' share in this partnership is governed by s.22B. If the partnership is chargeable to profits tax for any year of assessment and has not received a tax return form, it is required to inform the IRD that the partnership is so chargeable (s.51(2)). The filing of tax returns is closely monitored by the IRD and enforcement action is taken in cases of non-compliance (see more details in section *A.1.6* below). Moreover, the IRD reports that, from time to time, it issues tax returns to partnerships that carry on business in Hong Kong or are limited partnerships formed under the laws of Hong Kong but with no profits chargeable to tax to review their tax positions. The IRD reports that the review process is on-going. Partnerships' tax affairs are reviewed at least once in every four years. Specific cases (e.g. loss making entities) are subject to more frequent reviews. The review cycle covers all partnerships with no profits chargeable to tax, except those that have reported the cessation of business, as this triggers the dissolution of the partnership. Tax returns for partnerships include the following information:

- names and addresses of partners;
- partners' Hong Kong Identity Card numbers or business registration numbers if the partners are companies;
- date on which the partners entered and left the partnership during the basis period; and
- profit and loss sharing ratio of partners.

155. Tax returns are retained by the IRD for ten years after the year of assessment to which the return relates. Where a partnership has been dissolved, the retention period is seven years.

Information held by service providers

156. In addition to information maintained by the Business Registration Office, the Companies Registry and the IRD, financial institutions (banks, securities firms and insurance institutions) and lawyers are required to maintain ownership and identity information, including beneficial ownership information, of the partners in a partnership obtained during CDD. The verification of the identity of beneficial owners is subject to a 25% threshold in regular cases and a 10% threshold in high-risk cases (Schedule 2, ss.1, 2(2) and 15). The term "beneficial owner" is defined in the AMLO and differs according to the particular legal entity or arrangement concerned (Schedule 1, s. 1). In relation to a partnership it means an individual who (A) is entitled to or controls, directly or indirectly, not less than a 10% share of the capital or profits of the partnership; (B) is, directly or indirectly, entitled to exercise or control the exercise of not less than 10% of the voting rights in the partnership; or (C) exercises ultimate control over the management of the partnership; or *(ii)* if the partnership is acting on behalf of another person, means the other person. Ownership information must be maintained throughout the continuance of the business relationship with a partnership and for a period of six years after the business relationship has ended (see section A.1.1 above).

Information held by the partnership or partners

157. There is no specific requirement for general or limited partnerships to maintain information on the identity of their partners. However, knowledge of the identity of partners is likely given the joint and several liability that rests on partners of general partnerships and general partners of limited partnerships. It is also necessary for partners to maintain this information in order to comply with the registration and tax filing obligations of the partnership.

Conclusion

158. Information is available to Hong Kong's competent authority that identifies the partners in any partnership that has income, deductions or credits for Hong Kong tax purposes, carries on business in Hong Kong, or is a limited partnership formed under Hong Kong law. Such partnerships are obliged to provide an annual partnership return to Hong Kong's Inland Revenue Department (IRD) identifying all partners in the partnership. The *Limited Partnership Ordinance* (s. 2) applies to limited partnerships formed

under Hong Kong law that are carrying on business in Hong Kong. As these limited partnerships carry on business, they are subject to tax filing obligations. In addition, the Companies Registry maintains a public register of all Hong Kong limited partnerships identifying all general and limited partners. In practice, most requests for information on the identity of partners of general partnerships carrying on business in Hong Kong or limited partnerships formed under the laws of Hong Kong can be answered after consulting the databases maintained by the IRD/Companies Registry. The Hong Kong authorities are also able to obtain information from the relevant partnership directly if necessary.

159. During the three-year period under review, Hong Kong received one request relating to the identity of partners in a partnership. The Hong Kong authorities accessed information from the IRD database to reply to this request.

Trusts (ToR A.1.4)

160. Trusts are recognised in Hong Kong's common law and statute law. The trust law regime in Hong Kong is mainly based on English common law. The United Kingdom trust concepts, such as the characteristics and formal requirements of trusts as well as trustees' duties under common law, are applicable in Hong Kong (*Basic Law* Art. 8).

161. Hong Kong's courts adjudicate cases in accordance with the laws applicable in Hong Kong, which includes common law concepts and principles (Basic Law Art. 84). The laws of Hong Kong after 1 July 1997 are the Basic Law, the laws previously in force (i.e. common law, rules of equity, ordinances, subordinate legislation and customary law) that are not incompatible with the Basic Law, and laws enacted by the legislature of Hong Kong since 1 July 1997. Hong Kong courts may refer to precedents of other common law jurisdictions (Basic Law Art. 84). Those precedents have a persuasive effect. The power of final adjudication is vested in Hong Kong's Court of Final Appeal, which replaced the former role of the Privy Council in London (Basic Law Art. 82). The Court of Final Appeal can invite judges of other common law jurisdictions to sit on it and hear cases.

162. Under common law, a trust arises wherever a person (a trustee) has control over property for the benefit of some other persons (beneficiaries) or for some objects permitted by law (e.g. charitable purposes), in such a way that the real benefit of the property accrues, not to the trustee, but to the beneficiaries or objects of the trust. Under common law, a valid trust requires three certainties: certainty of intention by the settlor to create a trust; certainty of trust property; and certainty of objects. In addition, a trust must be completely constituted. If trust property consists of real estate, whether with

a legal or an equitable interest, the declaration of the trust has to be in writing (*Conveyancing and Property Ordinance* (Cap.219 s. 5(1)(b)). Other types of trusts capable of being created under the laws of Hong Kong include unit trusts (as well as other collective investment schemes constituted in the form of trusts such as pooled retirement funds and real estate investment trusts); and mandatory provident fund schemes and occupational retirement schemes.

163. Hong Kong's common law principles in relation to trusts have been modified by the following legislation: *Trustee Ordinance* (Cap.29); *Perpetuities and Accumulations Ordinance* (Cap.257); *Wills Ordinance* (Cap.30); *Recognition of Trusts Ordinance* (Cap.76) and the *Variation of Trusts Ordinance* (Cap. 253). Further, Hong Kong is a party to the *Convention on the Law Applicable to Trusts and on Their Recognition* (1985) (the Hague Convention) and provisions of the Hague Convention apply to Hong Kong by virtue of the *Recognition of Trusts Ordinance* (Cap. 76).

164. The *Trustee Ordinance* was enacted to supplement and amend the common law rules relating to trustees. It is modelled on the *English Trustee Act* of 1925. The powers conferred by the *Trustee Ordinance* on trustees apply to a trust if, and so far only as, a contrary intention is not expressed in the instrument creating the trust (s. 3). The *Trustee Ordinance* provides that settlement and dispositions on trust for the sale of land may have no more than four trustees (s. 36), which may include trust companies. Trustees appointed by certain bodies of persons or charities may be (not obligatory) incorporated under the *Registered Trustees Incorporation Ordinance* as registered trustee corporations. Registered trustee corporations are required to submit their particulars to the Companies Registry.

165. Unit trusts and other trusts that are offered to the public in Hong Kong are subject to financial licensing and regulation. Unit trusts are obliged to appoint a trustee acceptable to the Securities and Futures Commission as required by the *Code on Unit Trusts and Mutual Funds* (Chapter 4). The trustee of a unit trust must be a bank licensed under the *Banking Ordinance* (s. 16), a trust company which is a subsidiary of such a bank, or a banking institution or trust company incorporated outside Hong Kong which is acceptable to the Securities and Futures Commission. Other collective investment schemes (as defined under the *Securities and Futures Ordinance*) constituted in the form of trusts such as pooled retirement funds and real estate investment trusts are also subject to similar requirements on the appointment of trustee.

166. As at 31 March 2013, there were 305 Securities and Futures Commission-authorised unit trusts domiciled in Hong Kong and the total net asset value of these unit trusts was EUR 42.47 billion as at 31 December 2012. There were 9 Securities and Futures Commission-authorised real estate

investment trusts domiciled in Hong Kong with a total market capitalisation of EUR 17.06 billion as at 31 December 2012.

167. For mandatory provident fund schemes, a company or a natural person may apply to the Mandatory Provident Fund Schemes Authority for approval as a trustee if they meet certain requirements contained in the *Mandatory Provident Fund Schemes Ordinance* (s. 20) and the *Mandatory Provident Fund Schemes (General) Regulation* (s. 16). For a company applicant, it must, *inter alia*, be a trust company registered under Part VIII of the *Trustee Ordinance* (if the company applicant is incorporated in Hong Kong) or be, *inter alia*, a company to which Part XI of the *Companies Ordinance* applies and the objects of which must contain some of, but not more than, those specified in section 81 of the *Trustee Ordinance* (s. 17) (if the company applicant is incorporated outside Hong Kong).

168. All mandatory provident fund schemes are collective investment schemes. The constituent funds of a mandatory provident fund scheme may invest in approved pooled investment funds (APIFs) that are either unit trusts or insurance policies. As at 31 December 2012, there were 41 mandatory provident fund schemes, 464 constituent funds, and 300 APIFs (of which 287 were unit trusts). As at 31 December 2012, the aggregate net asset value of all mandatory provident fund schemes was HKD 439 839 million (EUR 43 419 million).

169. Charitable trusts may apply to the IRD for recognition as tax-exempt charities (Inland Revenue Ordinance s. 88). For charitable trusts recognised under s. 88 (tax-exempt status), the IRD maintains certain information about the trusts, which includes its governing instruments (trust deed) and documents recording its activities. A list of charitable entities, including charitable trusts recognised as tax-exempt charities (s. 88), is available on the IRD website.[22] A charitable trust not recognised as a tax-exempt charity is obliged to submit annual tax returns to the IRD for assessment similar to other business entities in Hong Kong. Some charitable bodies may also register with the Companies Registry under the *Registered Trustees Incorporation Ordinance* as registered trustee corporations.

170. There are no apparent prohibitions for a resident of Hong Kong to act as a trustee or otherwise in a fiduciary capacity in relation to a trust formed in Hong Kong or under foreign law. Likewise, there are no apparent prohibitions for a resident of Hong Kong from administering a trust or acting as a protector of a trust governed under foreign law. Under the common law, a person (natural or legal) who is of full legal capacity may act as a trustee.

22. Accessible at: www.ird.gov.hk/eng/pdf/e_s88list_emb.pdf.

Registration and licensing requirements of trusts and trustees

171. There is no general register of trusts in Hong Kong, though there is a voluntary register of trust companies under Part VIII of the *Trustee Ordinance* (ss.77-108).

172. Registered trustee companies under the *Registered Trustees Incorporation Ordinance* are required to submit the following information together with their application for registration with the Companies Registry: the nature and objects of the corporation; its rules and regulations; copies of every deed and other instruments constituting the corporation; descriptions of all properties held by the corporation; the names, residential addresses, occupations and nationalities of the trustees of the corporation; the address of the principal office; and details of the common seal and regulations for the custody and use thereof (Schedule 1).

173. The Companies Registry maintains a register of trustee corporations that choose to voluntarily register and all documents submitted with the applications for incorporation. The information is available to members of the public. Notice of any change in the address of the principal office or the appointment of any new trustee and the death, resignation or removal of any trustee must be given with 28 days of the change to the Companies Registry (*Registered Trustees Incorporation Ordinance* s. 9).

174. For unit trusts, real estate investment trusts and pooled retirement funds (in the form of a trust) offered to the public in Hong Kong, applicants must complete and submit the relevant application forms and information checklists to the Securities and Futures Commission for an application for authorisation. The offering documents and constitutive documents of the unit trusts, real estate investment trusts, pooled retirement funds (in the form of trusts) must comply with the relevant requirements under the applicable product codes and guidelines issued by the Securities and Futures Commission. The relevant application forms and information checklists contain *inter alia* the identity of the management company and the trustee of the unit trust, real estate investment trusts and pooled retirement funds (in the form of trusts). It is an offence under the *Securities and Futures Ordinance* if the offering documents of a collective investment scheme (whether it is constituted in the form of a unit trust, real estate investment trust, pooled retirement fund or other trusts) are issued to the public in Hong Kong unless the issue is authorised by the Securities and Futures Commission, or an exemption applies (s. 103).

Taxation of trusts

175. The *Inland Revenue Ordinance* provides that profits tax is charged on every person carrying on a trade, profession or business in Hong Kong in respect of his or her assessable profits arising in or derived from Hong Kong (s. 14(1)). The income of a trust derived from a trade, profession or business carried on in Hong Kong is chargeable on the trustee of the trust as the definition of "person" in the *Inland Revenue Ordinance* includes a trustee (s. 2). In such a case, the trustee, like other persons carrying on businesses in Hong Kong, is required to furnish profits tax returns with the IRD. After the trustee has been charged to tax, distributions to beneficiaries of trusts are not taxable in Hong Kong. Since capital expenditure, dividends and interest expenses are not deductible for profits tax purpose, capital gains, dividends and interest income are not subject to profits tax in Hong Kong. As a result, if a trust simply holds shares as a capital investment on which it earns dividends, the trust, trustee or beneficiaries will not be subject to Hong Kong profits tax on that income. Income derived by the trust from assets located outside Hong Kong is not taxable to the trustee, the trust or the beneficiaries under Hong Kong's territorial system. In the cases where no tax obligation arises in Hong Kong, as described above, there are generally no tax reporting requirements, although the trustees are obliged to answer any questions from the IRD concerning settlors or beneficiaries of a trust.

176. Charitable trusts of a public character are exempt from tax pursuant to the *Inland Revenue Ordinance* (s. 88). To be recognised as a tax-exempt charity, a charitable trust must furnish the IRD its trust deed to demonstrate that its objects are exclusively charitable according to the law, such as relief of poverty, advancement of education, *etc*. Once the tax exemption status is recognised, the charity is not required to file a tax return. Hong Kong authorities report, however, that the IRD will, from time to time, call for accounts, annual reports or other documents to review the tax exemption status and to examine whether the charity's objects remain charitable and its activities are compatible with the objects. Charitable trusts are also required to notify the IRD of any alteration of its governing instrument, i.e. its trust deed, to ensure that it remains exclusively charitable.

177. There is no requirement under the *Inland Revenue Ordinance* for filing of information by a trust regarding the identity of settlors, trustees and beneficiaries to the IRD. In the event a charitable trust applies to the IRD for recognition of its exemption status, the identity of the settlors and trustees will be found in the trust deed which is required to be supplied by the charitable trust in support of its application. For charitable trusts, typically no individual beneficiary will be named in the trust deed.

Identity information maintained by trustees

178. In Hong Kong, it is fundamental for an express trust to be properly constituted and that there be a settlor and trustee(s). A trust instrument will contain the information on the identity of the settlor and trustee(s). There is also an implicit common law requirement in Hong Kong to include information on the identities of beneficiaries in the trust instrument. For a trust created in writing, the writing, although required only as evidence of the declaration of the trust, must contain all material terms of the trust. The beneficiaries must be expressly designated or so defined that they are capable of being ascertained, otherwise the trust is void for uncertainty.[23] Hong Kong authorities report that it is common for trusts to be created in writing in Hong Kong.

179. In Hong Kong, trustees have a common law obligation to properly administer the trust, to act impartially in the execution of the trust, and not to exercise his or her power so as to confer an advantage on one beneficiary at the expense of other beneficiaries.[24] There are other specific common law duties that a trustee must comply with. For example, trustees owe beneficiaries a duty of care in the investment of trust funds, appointment of agents, and administration of trust property.[25] Additionally, trustees are under a common law duty to strictly conform to and carry out the terms of the trust, in so far as they are in force.[26] Trustees owe fiduciary duties to beneficiaries and are liable for a breach of such duties.[27]

180. For unit trusts and real estate investment trusts, the trustee, or the person so appointed by the trustee, is obliged to maintain a register in Hong Kong of unit holders (*Securities and Futures Ordinance* s. 336). Unit trusts are obliged to inform the Securities and Futures Commission of the address(es) where the register is kept (s. 336). For provident fund schemes, the information on employers (settlors) held by a trustee includes the name and contact details of the employers and, in the case of a self-employed person, the Hong Kong identity card or passport number. The information on employees (beneficiaries) held by a trustee includes the names and contact details of the employees (*Mandatory Provident Fund Schemes Ordinance* s. 139).

181. For occupational retirement schemes, while there is no statutory requirement on what information a trustee is required to have regarding

---

23. *Re Baden's Deed Trust* (No. 2) [1973] Ch. 9.
24. *Edge v Pensions Ombudsman* [2000] Ch. 602 at 618.
25. *Speigh v Gaunt* (1883) 9 App Cas 1.
26. *AG v Lady Downing* (1767) Wilm 1 at 23-25; *Booth v Booth* (1838) 1 Beav 125 at 128-129; *Knott v Cottee* (1852) 16 Beav 77; Halsbury's Laws of Hong Kong, Vol 26(2), 2009 Reissue, at 400.522.
27. *Lai Kit Bick & Another v To Yui Hung,* 2004 HKEC 1576).

the identity of a settlor or beneficiary, the identity and contact details of the relevant employer (settlor) would be known to the trustee in order for him to discharge his or her duties under the occupational retirement scheme. Similarly, the trustee would require the following information on the identity of the beneficiary (the employee) in order for him or her to discharge their duties under the occupational retirement scheme: name of the employee, contact details, employer's and employee's contributions and amount of accrued benefits.

182. There is an implicit common law requirement in Hong Kong that a trustee should have knowledge of all documents pertaining to the formation of the trust and it is a common law requirement that a trustee should have knowledge of all the documents pertaining to the management of the trust. A trustee also has a common law duty to keep accounts and records of the trust and to produce them to beneficiaries when required. In short, a trustee is under a common law duty to keep all such information and records of the trust to ensure that he or she can perform their duties as trustee properly. A trustee also has a duty under the common law to obey the lawful directions of a settlement, except in so far as these directions are modified by all the beneficiaries or by the court; such directions may be found in the documents pertaining to the formation of the trust.

Identity information maintained by service providers

183. Lawyers and financial institutions are the only providers of trust services which are required to conduct CDD on the trust for which they work. Lawyers and financial institutions (banks and other deposit-taking companies) are obliged to identify and verify the beneficial owners of trusts and other legal arrangements which are their customers. Paragraph 93 of the *Law Society's Practice Direction* provides that where the client itself or the transaction to be undertaken involves trust arrangements, the lawyers must take reasonable steps to identify all parties involved, including the trustee, settlor and beneficiaries. Guidelines issued by the respective regulator or professional body set out the CDD requirements for trust and nominee accounts.

184. Financial institutions are required to obtain satisfactory evidence of the identity of the trustees, protectors, settlors and beneficiaries, and understand the details of the nature of the trust and the relationship between the various parties. In practice, the following documents are accepted as satisfactory evidence: copy of the trust deed, copy of the trust registration certificate, statement by a trustee confirming he or she is acting as such in a professional capacity, a statement from a lawyer confirming that he or she had access to the trust deed. Financial institutions may rely in certain circumstances on CDD performed by intermediaries specified in the *AMLO*. Financial institutions that carry out a CDD through an intermediary remain liable under the

AMLO for failure to carry out CDD. According to section 18(3) of Schedule 2 of the *AMLO*, the intermediaries are any of the following persons who are able to satisfy the financial institution that they have adequate procedures in place to prevent money laundering and terrorist financing (a) a solicitor practising in Hong Kong; (b) a certified public accountant practising in Hong Kong; (c) a current member of the Hong Kong Institute of Chartered Secretaries practising in Hong Kong; (d) a trust company registered under the Trustee Ordinance (Cap. 29) carrying on trust business in Hong Kong.

185. The *AMLO* (effective 1 April 2012) imposes statutory CDD and record-keeping requirements on financial institutions. Under the *AMLO*, CDD requirements include the identification and verification of the identities of customers and their beneficial owners (if any). In relation to a trust, the *AMLO* includes the following definition of beneficial owners (s. 1(1)(c), Schedule 2):

- an individual who is entitled to a vested interest in not less than 10% of the capital of the trust property, whether the interest is in possession or in remainder or reversion and whether it is defeasible or not;[28]
- the settlor of the trust;
- a protector or enforcer of the trust; or
- an individual who has ultimate control over the trust.

186. Hong Kong authorities report that local trustees of foreign express trusts typically conduct business with financial institutions in Hong Kong. When local trustees conduct business with financial institutions in Hong Kong, the financial institutions are required under the *AMLO* to conduct CDD on the trustees. The identity and ownership information of foreign express trusts should then be available and maintained by financial institutions. There are, however, no legal requirements for trustees in Hong Kong to conduct business with financial institutions in Hong Kong. Thus, it is recommended that Hong Kong monitor the availability of ownership and identity information for foreign express trusts having a resident trustee(s) in Hong Kong, in particular any EOI requests that cannot be satisfied because the information is not maintained.

28. Notwithstanding the above, pursuant to section 2 Schedule 2 of the AMLO, a higher threshold (of 25%) is established in connection with regular CDD obligations of financial institutions. That is to say, except in cases considered as high risk cases by the regulators, financial institutions are not required to verify the identity of individuals that hold a vested interest of less than 25% of the capital of the relevant trust property, whether the interest is in possession or in remainder or reversion and whether it is defeasible or not (ss.2 (2) and 15).

187. Financial institutions and lawyers are required to keep information or documents obtained during CDD throughout the continuance of the business relationship with a trust and for a period of six years beginning on the date on which the business relationship ends. In the case of licensed corporations, records on customer identification should be kept for at least six years after the account is closed.

188. Licensed corporations (including a management company licensed by the Securities and Futures Commission of a unit trust) are required under the *Securities and Futures (Keeping of Records) Rules* to keep records as are sufficient to, among others, explain the operation of its business and account for all client assets enabling them to be traced through its accounting system and, where applicable, stock holding systems including documents evidencing authorities provided by clients, written agreements with clients, *etc* (s. 3). These records must be retained for not less than seven years. Licensed corporations must obtain the prior written approval from the Securities and Futures Commission in order to use any premises for the keeping of records or documents relating to the carrying on of the regulated activity for which it is licensed (*Securities and Futures Ordinance* s. 130).

189. As for trust service providers, the Hong Kong Trustees' Association (HKTA), which is a professional organisation in Hong Kong with approximately 100 members representing thousands of professionals working in the trust, private banking, fund services, legal and accounting sectors, issued Best Practice Guides to its members in August 2012. The Best Practice Guides highlight the fiduciary duty of trustees to know their customer. The Best Practice Guides do not have the force of law and are not mandatory. The HKTA is not a regulatory body and does not currently monitor its members' compliance with the guides.

Funds

190. Collective investment funds established under Hong Kong law include trusts (including unit trusts), limited liability companies and limited partnerships.

191. Generally, however, they are established as unit trusts. Unit trusts are governed by the provisions of the trust deeds under which they are constituted and are subject to general trust law. Offers of interests in CIS to the public in Hong Kong require prior authorisation from the SFC under the *Securities and Futures Ordinance* (s. 104). Fund managers may also choose to set up CIS offshore. The SFC may authorise the offering of offshore CIS provided that they are domiciled in jurisdictions recognised by the SFC or otherwise comply with applicable SFC regulations. As at 31 December 2012, around 56% of the SFC-authorised funds were domiciled in Luxembourg, 16.6% in Hong

Kong and 15.1% in Ireland. Other places of domicile for the funds include, for example, the UK, the Cayman Islands, the British Virgin Islands, Bermuda and Guernsey. The SFC has issued codes such as the Code on Unit Trusts and Mutual Funds, the SFC Code on Mandatory Provident Funds Products and the Code on Pooled Retirement Funds which must be complied with by the relevant types of authorised CIS. Listed CIS are also subject to Listing Rules of the Stock Exchange of Hong Kong. The total number of SFC-authorised funds as of 31 March 2013 is 1 847 with total net asset value of USD 1 237 billion as at 31 December 2012.

192. In addition to the authorisation of CIS offered to the public, the SFC also regulates asset management companies. A management company that carries out asset management activities in Hong Kong must be licensed by the SFC. An overseas management company managing these CIS must be subject to the oversight of a regulator in an acceptable inspection regime.

193. According to the Code on Unit Trusts and Mutual Funds, the trustee or a person appointed by the trustee must maintain a register of holders. In other words, the trustee must maintain or cause to maintain a register with details of all registered unit holders in whose name the units are subscribed/held. All unitised funds must have a register that keeps unit holder/shareholder records and processes subscription, redemption, switching, transfer and makes redemption payment to the unit holder/shareholder. For collective investment funds, unit holders/shareholders of the fund own units in the funds and proper accounting record (including processing of subscription/redemption and transfers) must be kept by the registrar or the transfer agency.

194. In addition, all distributors in Hong Kong must hold a relevant licence before making fund distributions. The following general requirements apply to fund subscription made via distributors:

- when distributors subscribe on behalf of their clients for units registered in the name of the distributors, the AML/CDD is performed on the distributor entity itself according to the requirements of the *AMLO*. The distributor being a licensed/regulated entity in Hong Kong is required to perform AML/CDD on their own customers (i.e. the investors) in accordance with the relevant provisions of the *AMLO*; or
- when distributors subscribe on behalf of their customers (i.e. the investors) and establish accounts that specify sub-accounts for named underlying investors, then in addition to the AML/CDD performed on the distributor, the identification documentation of the named underlying investors must also be obtained in accordance with the *AMLO* requirements applicable to that investor category.

195. These requirements also apply to situation where "omnibus accounts" or "nominees' accounts" are used by an intermediary subscribing on behalf of their customers (i.e. underlying investors).

Conclusion

196. Under common law, a trust created in writing must contain all material terms of the trust, including identification of the settlor(s), trustee(s), and beneficiary(ies). If trust property consists of real estate, whether with a legal or an equitable interest, the declaration of the trust has to be in writing. It is common but not mandatory for other trusts to be created in writing in Hong Kong. Trustees have common law obligations including the obligations to properly administer the trust and to not confer an advantage on one beneficiary at the expense of other beneficiaries. Additionally, trustees are under a common law duty to strictly conform to and carry out the terms of the trust, and they owe fiduciary duties to beneficiaries.

197. Unit trusts and other trusts that are offered to the public in Hong Kong are subject to regulation to provide for identification of trustees, settlors and beneficiaries. Lawyers and banking, securities and insurance institutions which have trusts as their customers are required to identify the beneficiaries of the trusts in accordance with AML obligations.

198. The scope of common law obligations is particularly relevant where there are gaps in statutory requirements to maintain ownership information for trusts. In Hong Kong, professional trustees (other than trustees of unit trusts and other trusts that are offered to the public) that are not financial institutions, lawyers and neither licensed nor subject to AML rules are only subject to Hong Kong's common law obligations, as modified by statutory provisions (e.g. *Trustee Ordinance* (Cap.29); *Perpetuities and Accumulations Ordinance* (Cap.257); *Wills Ordinance* (Cap.30); *Recognition of Trusts Ordinance* (Cap.76) and the *Variation of Trusts Ordinance* (Cap. 253)).

199. In practice, the Hong Kong authorities indicate that many trustees of private express trusts and foreign trusts are financial institutions or lawyers who are subject to the AML/CFT regulatory regime and are accordingly obliged to conduct CDD. It is possible, however, that there exist professional trust companies acting as trustees that are not subject to AML/CFT requirements. The Hong Kong authorities also indicate that, most trustees administering trusts with significant assets will use the services of financial institutions and lawyers in connection with those trusts. The authorities consider that ownership and identity information on these trusts will, therefore, be made available to the financial institutions and lawyers concerned. Moreover, the Hong Kong authorities consider that, in the unlikely event that the trustees are not clients of financial institutions or lawyers, those trustees

remain subject to common law obligations to maintain all documents pertaining to the formation and management of trusts. The Hong Kong authorities are of the view that a trust instrument will contain information on the identity of settlors and beneficiaries. Hence, the Hong Kong authorities are of the view that ownership and identity information in respect of trusts is available through a combination of AML and common law requirements.

200. It is noted, however, that, in circumstances where *(i)* trustees of private express trusts or foreign trusts are not Hong Kong financial institutions or lawyers, and *(ii)* the trust neither carries on business in Hong Kong *(iii)* nor engages financial institutions or lawyers in Hong Kong, there appears to be no specific regulatory oversight or monitoring of whether these trustees maintain information and documents pertaining to the management of trusts, including ownership information.

201. Tax reporting requirements are imposed on trustees of trusts carrying on business in Hong Kong. If a trust is not carrying on business and, for example, simply holds shares for investment purposes on which it earns dividends, such dividends are not taxable in Hong Kong and there are no reporting requirements. Income derived by the trust from assets located outside Hong Kong is not taxable to the trustee, the trust or the beneficiaries under Hong Kong's territorial system. The Hong Kong authorities report that trustees are, nevertheless, obliged to answer enquiries from the IRD regarding any information and documentation relevant to the management of trusts, or concerning the identification of settlors and beneficiaries of the trust.

202. There are no obstacles preventing Hong Kong residents from acting as trustees or administrators of foreign trusts. Foreign trusts are governed by foreign law (including common law), so it is unclear what statutory or common law obligations would apply with respect to these arrangements. Since Hong Kong is a signatory to the *Hague Convention*, the law of the jurisdiction in which the trust was established would generally be recognised and applied. It is conceivable that certain aspects of the common law may not be applicable in that jurisdiction or even that the jurisdiction is a civil law one. Moreover, certain aspects of Hong Kong's common law may conflict with the common law of the jurisdiction governing the trust. In any event, even where the common law applies, the question remains whether there is sufficient oversight by a Hong Kong government authority on whether information or documents are being kept in all cases.

203. In summary, the concern remains whether Hong Kong resident trustees of private express trusts systematically keep documentation that identifies settlors and beneficiaries of the trust in all circumstances. It is recommended that a statutory obligation be established to maintain information in all cases in relation to settlors, trustees and beneficiaries of trusts with a trustee in Hong Kong. Given the significant size of the trust sector in Hong

Kong and its potential relevance to EOI with other jurisdictions, Hong Kong should monitor whether Hong Kong resident trustees maintain information that identifies the settlors and beneficiaries of the trust in all cases.

204. During the three-year period under review, Hong Kong did not receive any requests concerning trustees, settlors or beneficiaries of trusts.

Foundations (ToR A.1.5)

205. There are no laws or common law principles that govern the establishment of foundations in Hong Kong. The term "foundation" is a categorisation used for not for profit entities usually formed as a trust or a non-profit company limited by guarantee for the purposes of relief of poverty, advancement of education, advancement of religion or other purposes beneficial to the community.

Enforcement provisions to ensure availability of information (ToR A.1.6)

206. The existence of appropriate penalties for non-compliance with key obligations is an important tool for jurisdictions to effectively enforce the obligations to retain identity and ownership information.

207. Companies incorporated in Hong Kong, non-Hong Kong companies with an established place of business in Hong Kong, and limited partnerships are obliged to register with the Companies Registry. Failure to comply with the registration requirements or to update registered particulars, is an offence and every officer of the company or general partners of the limited partnership who are in default are liable to a fine between level three (HKD 10 000) (EUR 987) and level five (HKD 50 000) (EUR 4936) and a daily default fine between HKD 300 (EUR 30) and HKD 700 (EUR 69) (*Companies Ordinance* Twelfth Schedule). For limited partnerships registered under the *Limited Partnership Ordinance,* there is a default daily fine of HKD 50 (EUR 5) (*Limited Partnership Ordinance* s. 8(2)).

208. As described in A.1.1, the Companies Registry has an automated system to monitor the filing of annual returns. The system automatically detects which companies fail to file annual returns by the due date. Companies that are in default of their obligations receive a notice and are given a period of 28 days from the date of the notice to rectify the default. Compliance is generally high. For annual returns required to be filed in 2012, 87.97% Hong Kong companies and 94.62% of non-Hong Kong companies complied with their filing obligations.

209. Subsequent actions against companies in default are taken, including sending reminders, making enquiries, initiating prosecution actions and

striking off actions. These follow up actions may, depending on the time of default in the year and circumstances of the case, not necessarily take place in the same year but the following year(s). Summonses for prosecution are issued if annual returns remain outstanding after the expiry of the 28-day grace period. In 2012, 6 209 Hong Kong companies and 86 non-Hong Kong companies were prosecuted by the Registrar for non-compliance with their annual filing obligations. The Companies Registry strikes off defunct companies from the register (i.e. companies that are not carrying on business or that are no longer in operation). Companies are considered to be defunct companies if they continuously fail to file annual returns. The Hong Kong authorities informed that, subject to the facts and circumstances of the individual case, normally a company is considered as defunct if it is in continuous default of filing annual returns for three years. In 2012, approximately 28 000 companies were struck off.

210. In practice, the Companies Registry investigates a limited partnership only when a complaint is filed by a third party (e.g. a partner or former partner). The Companies Registry reports that during the period under review it has not received any complaints concerning limited partnerships' compliance with their filing obligations under the *Limited Partnership Ordinance.* Monitoring of partnerships' tax filing obligations is carried out by the IRD.

211. In addition, under section 349 of the *Companies Ordinance,* any person who wilfully makes a false statement in any return, certificate or other document to the Companies Registry is guilty of an offence and liable to a fine at level six (HKD 100 000) (EUR 8 897) and imprisonment for six months. During the three-year period under review, there was one conviction under this section.

212. If any company incorporated in Hong Kong fails to maintain registers required to be maintained under the *Companies Ordinance*, the company and every officer of the company who is in default is liable to a fine and, for continued default, to a daily default fine. Particulars of the sanctions for non-compliance under the *Companies Ordinance* are as follows:

Section	General nature of offence	Punishment	Daily default fine
89(4)	Failing to keep a register of charges or failing to notify the Registrar where the register of charges is kept.	Level 5 (HKD 50 000) (EUR 4 936)	HKD 700 (EUR 69)
95(4)	Failing to keep a register of members or failing to notify the Registrar of place where register is kept.	Level 4 (HKD 25 000) (EUR 2 468)	HKD 700
158A(2)	Failing to keep a register of directors and secretaries at registered office or failing to notify the Registrar of place where register is kept.	Level 5 (HKD 50 000)	HKD 700

213. During the three-year period under review, there was one conviction under this subsection 89(4), two convictions under subsection 95(4) and one conviction under subsection 158A(2).

214. Under the *Securities and Futures Ordinance*, it is a criminal offence if a person, without reasonable excuse, fails to make a disclosure in accordance with the provisions of Part XV (e.g. disclosure of substantial shareholders) that apply to that disclosure, or when making a disclosure, makes a statement that is knowingly false or misleading in a material particular (ss.328 and 351). If a person commits an offence they are liable on conviction on indictment to a fine of level 6 (HKD 100 000) (EUR 9 872) and to imprisonment for two years; or on summary conviction to a fine of level three (HKD 10 000) (EUR 987) and to imprisonment for six months for each offence of which he or she is convicted (ss. 328, 351). During the three-year period under review, there were 29 successful prosecutions in relation to the disclosure of interests for which fines were imposed of more than HKD 10 000.

215. Under the *Business Registration Ordinance*, any person who fails to make application for registration, or fails to notify the Business Registration Office of any change in particulars, or makes any statement or furnishes any information which is false is guilty of an offence and liable to a fine at level two (HKD 5 000) (EUR 494) and to imprisonment for 1 year (s. 15). In respect of the failure to make application for registration or to notify the Business Registration Office of any change in particulars, the magistrate may, in addition to any penalty that may be imposed, order that the person shall within a time specified in the order do the act which he has failed to do (s. 15(1A)).

216. The IRD has a programme of on-site inspections and has identified cases of failure to register a business. Its active programme monitors compliance with legal requirements and it has instituted prosecutions when non-compliance was detected. Approximately 15 000 to 20 000 on-site visits were conducted each year from 2009 to 2012. Approximately 2 500-4 000 prosecutions took place each year from 2009 to 2012 in connection with the failure to register a business in Hong Kong.

217. The *Inland Revenue Ordinance* provides that failure to file any return required to be filed pursuant to section 51(1) or 51(2) is an offence and subjects the person and its representatives to a fine at level three (HKD 10 000) (EUR 987) and a further fine of treble the amount of tax which was undercharged if such failure had not been detected (s. 80). Taxpayers are obliged to declare in their return that all the particulars contained in the return are true, correct, and complete. Any person who without reasonable excuse makes an incorrect return by omitting anything in respect of which he or she is required to make, or makes an incorrect statement in connection with a claim for any deduction or allowance commits an offence and is liable on conviction

to a fine of HKD 10 000 and a further fine of treble the amount of tax which was undercharged in consequence of such incorrect return (s. 80(2)).

218. The IRD opens profits tax files for corporations and partnerships and individual tax files for sole-proprietorships. The IRD reports that newly formed or registered companies normally receive their first tax return 18 months after the date of commencement of business or the date of incorporation. Dormant companies are subject to periodic review instead of receiving an annual return (as a rule, they would receive the tax return within a time period not longer than 4 years).

219. The IRD closely monitors the filing of tax returns. When a taxpayer fails to submit a tax return within the stipulated time limit, the IRD reports that it takes follow up action such as issuing compound letters and writ of summons, before proceeding to initiate court action. The IRD reports that most taxpayers comply with their filing obligations upon receipt of these formal notices. For the remaining cases, the IRD would then initiate court action. Details concerning the fines imposed by the court in connection with the failure to file returns are summarised in the table below.[29]

Profits Tax – Court Fines Imposed – Failure to submit tax return (s. 80(1)&(2)(d))

Year of Assessment	Corporations		Unincorporated business (e.g. partnerships)	
	No. of convictions	Amount of Fines (HKD)	No. of convictions	Amount of Fines (HKD)
2009-10	10 018	21 887 700	455	864 800
2010-11	7 903	18 342 800	465	872 000
2011-12	7 826	18 963 450	493	1 070 100

220. Enforcement action is taken when taxpayers fail to comply with court orders, as summarised in the table below.

Profits Tax – Court Fines Imposed – Failure to comply with Court Order (s. 80(2B))

Year of Assessment	Corporations		Unincorporated business (e.g. partnerships)	
	No. of convictions	Amount of Fines (HKD)	No. of convictions	Amount of Fines (HKD)
2009-10	1 512	7 154 500	34	154 100
2010-11	921	4 843 950	19	107 400
2011-12	914	4 593 700	25	91 700

29. Statistics and amounts concerning late payment of tax, failure to comply with notices, imposition of additional tax and penalties for the submission of false returns with intent to evade tax are not included below.

221. Failure to give notice of any change as required under the *Registered Trustees Incorporation Ordinance* is an offence and subjects the trustee(s) to a fine of HKD 500 (EUR 49.36) on summary conviction (s. 9). There have not been any convictions during the three-year period under review.

222. Financial institutions, their employees or persons concerned in their management who breach the relevant CDD or record-keeping requirements are subject to prosecution. They are liable on conviction to a maximum fine of HKD 1 million (EUR 98 800) and to a maximum term of imprisonment of 7 years. Financial institutions are also subject to disciplinary action by relevant authorities. The disciplinary action includes publicly reprimanding the financial institution; ordering it to take remedial action; imposing fines not exceeding the greater of *(i)* HKD 10 million (EUR 0.988 million) or *(ii)* three times the amount of profit gained, or costs avoided, by the financial institution as a result of the contravention. The regulators have developed a programme of onsite and offsite examinations focusing on high-risk areas (e.g. thematic examinations on private banks).

223. Between April 2012 and March 2013, the HKMA conducted 23 AML/CFT specific on-site examinations on authorised institutions to review their compliance with supervisory requirements and directed improvements to be made where appropriate. For the securities sector, the SFC conducted 208 inspections (including an AML/CFT component) between April 2012 and March 2013. The SFC issued public reprimands to two entities, imposed fines on two entities and suspended/prohibited five entities from re-entering the industry. For the insurance sector, a total of 97 inspections were conducted between April 2012 and March 2013 to review operators' compliance with regulatory requirements and directed improvements to be made where appropriate.

224. Failure to observe the Law Society's practice direction on CDD obligations is treated as professional misconduct in respect of which disciplinary action may be taken (e.g. revocation or suspension of licence, payment of penalty) (chapter 16 *Hong Kong Solicitors' Guide to Professional Conduct)*. The Law Society reported that it is not aware of any breaches to date and hence it has not applied any sanctions in connection with the mandatory practice direction on AML/CFT to date. At present, the Law Society does not have a policy of carrying out routine checks on compliance with its practice direction on AML/CFT. The Law Society's investigation powers are instigated when irregularities and infringements are detected by compliance officers.

Conclusion and practice

225. Enforcement provisions are in place with respect to the relevant obligations to maintain ownership and identity information for relevant entities. The necessary tools exist to address non-compliance through a combination

of obligations under tax law, company law and regulatory laws. The applicable enforcement measures appear to be dissuasive enough to ensure compliance. Moreover, there appears to be adequate monitoring of compliance with most obligations to retain identity and ownership information. It is noted, however, that there is no statutory obligation on Hong Kong residents that act as trustees of private express trusts or foreign trusts, to keep documentation that identifies settlors and beneficiaries of private express trusts or foreign trusts.

226. Based on the peer input received, Hong Kong was capable of responding to all requests for ownership and identity information received from its peers. This indicates that ownership and identity information was effectively maintained in Hong Kong. During the period under review, Hong Kong did not receive any requests concerning trustees, settlors or beneficiaries of trusts.

Determination and factors underlying recommendations

Phase 1 determination	
The element is in place, but certain aspects of the legal implementation of the element need improvement.	
Factors underlying recommendations	**Recommendations**
Nominees that are not subject to AML obligations (i.e. those other than lawyers or financial institutions) are not required to maintain ownership and identity information in respect of all persons for whom they act as legal owners.	An obligation should be established for all nominees to maintain relevant ownership information where they act as the legal owners on behalf of any other persons.
While there are no share warrants to bearer in circulation at present, there are currently insufficient mechanisms in place that ensure the availability of information allowing for identification of their owners. The new *Companies Ordinance*, which has been enacted but is not yet in operation, repeals the power of a company to issue share warrants to bearer as of the day the ordinance becomes operative.	Hong Kong should continue to take necessary steps to ensure that robust mechanisms are in place to identify the owners of share warrants to bearer or eliminate companies' ability to issue such shares.

Phase 1 determination	
The element is in place, but certain aspects of the legal implementation of the element need improvement.	
Factors underlying recommendations	**Recommendations**
Not all trustees of private express trusts and foreign trusts are statutorily required to have information available on the identity of settlors and beneficiaries of trusts.	Hong Kong should ensure that information that identifies the settlors, trustees and beneficiaries of private express trusts and foreign trusts in respect of which a trustee is resident in Hong Kong, is available to its competent authority.

Phase 2 rating	
Partially Compliant	
Factors underlying recommendations	**Recommendations**
In circumstances where Hong Kong trustees of private express trusts or foreign trusts are not Hong Kong financial institutions or lawyers, and the trust neither carries on business in Hong Kong nor derives income which is taxable in Hong Kong, there is no systematic monitoring by government authorities of whether the trustees maintain information or documents pertaining to the identification of settlors and beneficiaries of these trusts.	Hong Kong should monitor whether Hong Kong trustees of private express trusts and foreign trusts maintain information that identifies the settlors and beneficiaries in all cases.

A.2. Accounting records

> Jurisdictions should ensure that reliable accounting records are kept for all relevant entities and arrangements.

227. The *Terms of Reference* sets out the standards for the maintenance of reliable accounting records and the necessary accounting record retention period. It provides that reliable accounting records should be kept for all relevant entities and arrangements. To be reliable, accounting records should: *(i)* correctly explain all transactions; *(ii)* enable the financial position of the entity or arrangement to be determined with reasonable accuracy at any time; and *(iii)* allow financial statements to be prepared. Accounting records should

further include underlying documentation, such as invoices, contracts, *etc.* Accounting records need to be kept for a minimum of five years.

General requirements (ToR A.2.1)

228. Accounting obligations in Hong Kong are primarily governed by the *Inland Revenue Ordinance* which has a broad scope, as well as specific ordinances governing particular types of legal entities and arrangements. The *Inland Revenue Ordinance* contains provisions requiring the maintenance of accounting records that correctly explain all transactions, enable the financial position of entities and arrangements to be determined with reasonable accuracy at any time, and allow financial statements to be prepared.

229. Every legal or natural person carrying on any trade, profession, or business[30] in Hong Kong (including foreign entities) is obliged to keep sufficient records in the English or Chinese language of its income (regardless of its source) and expenditure to enable the assessable profits of such trade, profession, or business to be readily ascertained (s. 51C(1)). The records prescribed in the *Ordinance* include (ss.51C(3) and (4)):

- books of account recording receipts and payments, or income and expenditure;
- underlying documentation such as vouchers, bank statements, invoices, receipts, and other documents necessary to verify the entries in the books of account;
- a record of assets and liabilities;
- a day-to-day record of all sums of money received and expended together with supporting details of the receipts or payments;
- (for taxpayers dealing in goods) a record of all sales and purchases of goods by the company, statements of trading stock and all records of stocktaking; and

30. The question of whether a business is carried on in Hong Kong and whether profits are derived from Hong Kong is largely one of fact; however decisions of the Hong Kong Courts and the Privy Council indicate that there is a very low threshold for a person to carry on business in Hong Kong. In the case of a company incorporated for the purpose of making profits for its shareholders, any gainful use to which it puts any of its assets prima facie amounts to carrying on business. The carrying on of business usually calls for some activity on the part of whoever carries it on, though, depending on the nature of the business, the activity may be intermittent with long intervals of quiescence in between. A company need not have extensive activities in Hong Kong before it is considered to be carrying on business in Hong Kong.

- (for taxpayers providing services) records of the services provided in sufficient detail to enable the IRD to readily verify the entries in the books of account.

230. Failure to maintain records is an offence and subject to a fine at level six (HKD 100 000) (EUR 9 872) and a court may order the person convicted to do the act which he or she has failed to do (s. 80(1A)). To assist the public in fulfilling their record keeping obligations, the IRD has published guidelines entitled "A Guide to Keeping Business Records".[31]

231. Moreover, any person chargeable to profits tax is required to furnish a completed tax return (*Inland Revenue Ordinance* s. 51(1)). The return must include details of the assessable profits or losses and be accompanied by a statement of the person's financial position/balance sheet and the profit and loss account.

232. Additional accounting record retention obligations are imposed in other ordinances that add to or reinforce the record-keeping requirements contained in the *Inland Revenue Ordinance*. These ordinances are specific to particular types of legal entities and arrangements and are detailed below.

Companies

233. The *Companies Ordinance* requires every company incorporated in Hong Kong to maintain proper books of account (s. 121). Proper books of account include records with respect to (s. 121):

- all sums of money received and expended and the matters in respect of which the receipt and expenditure take place;
- all sales and purchases of goods; and
- the assets and liabilities.

234. The books of account must give a true and fair view of the state of the company's affairs and explain its transactions (*Companies Ordinance* s. 121). The books of account of companies incorporated in Hong Kong must be kept at the registered office of the company or at such other place as the directors think fit. If they are kept at a place outside Hong Kong, returns which are sufficient to disclose the financial position of the company with reasonable accuracy must be sent and kept at a place in Hong Kong at intervals of not more than six months. They must also be sufficient to enable the company's accounts to be prepared (s. 121). Audited accounts are required for every company incorporated in Hong Kong (s. 141). The auditors' report must state whether, in their opinion, the balance sheet referred to in the report is

31. Accessible at: www.ird.gov.hk/eng/pdf/51c_pam.pdf.

properly drawn up so as to exhibit a true and correct view of the state of the company's affairs according to the best of their information and the explanations given to them, and as shown by the books of the company (ss. 141I and 141D). Pursuant to section 140(1) of the *Companies Ordinance,* a person cannot be appointed as auditor of a company unless he or she is qualified for appointment as such auditor under the *Professional Accountants Ordinance* (Cap.50).

235. Failure to take all reasonable steps to ensure that the company maintains proper books of account is an offence and subjects the company's directors on summary prosecution to imprisonment for 12 months and a fine of HKD 300 000 (EUR 29 615) (s. 121(4)). From 2009 to 2012, there were 393 convictions for the offence described above.

236. For companies incorporated outside of Hong Kong with a place of business in Hong Kong, the requirements within the *Companies Ordinance* for companies to keep accounts depends on the law of the jurisdiction in which the company was incorporated. That said, the *Companies Ordinance* requires a non-Hong Kong company to deliver a certified copy of its latest published accounts together with the annual return for registration with the Companies Registry if the company is required by the law of the place of its incorporation, the laws of other jurisdictions where the company is registered as a company, or the rules of any stock exchange or similar regulatory bodies in any of those jurisdictions to publish its accounts or to deliver copies of its accounts to any person in whose office they may be inspected (s. 336). In 2012, 94.62% of the registered non-Hong Kong companies complied with their filing obligations in a timely manner. In the same year, 86 non-Hong Kong companies were summoned for non-compliance with their filing obligations with the Companies Registry. Additionally, the Listing Rules of the Hong Kong Stock Exchange require all listed companies in Hong Kong, regardless of where they are incorporated, to prepare audited accounts. Non-Hong Kong companies carrying on any trade, profession, or business in Hong Kong are also subject to the accounting record obligations contained in the *Inland Revenue Ordinance* (*Inland Revenue Ordinance* s. 51C(1).

Partnerships

237. The *Inland Revenue Ordinance* defines "person" as including a partnership (s. 2). A "partnership" is defined under the *Partnership Ordinance* as "the relation which subsists between persons carrying on a business in common with a view of profit" (s. 3). Being persons carrying on a business, all partnerships in Hong Kong are chargeable to profits tax pursuant to the *Inland Revenue Ordinance* and are therefore required to keep sufficient accounting records (described above) as prescribed under section 51C (s. 14). Failure to comply with the record keeping requirement as stipulated under

section 51C of the *Inland Revenue Ordinance* is an offense and subject to a fine of HKD 100 000 (EUR 9 872) and a court may order the person convicted to do the act which he or she has failed to do within a specified time. During the period under review, the IRD reports that there were 110 penal actions taken in relation to partnerships.

238. Under the *Inland Revenue Ordinance*, the precedent partner of a partnership is answerable for keeping accounting records (s. 56). A "precedent partner" is defined as the partner who, of the active partners resident in Hong Kong, is first named in the agreement of partnership or specified in the usual name of the partnership (s. 2).

Trusts

239. If a trust carries on a trade, profession or business in Hong Kong, the requirements under the *Inland Revenue Ordinance* s. 51C(1), i.e. to keep sufficient records of its income and expenditure to enable the assessable profits to be readily ascertained, also apply. Whether a private express trust is considered to be carrying on a business by holding investments depends on the particular facts and circumstances. Factors taken into account include the frequency of transactions, the length in holding the assets in question, and the organisational set-up.

240. Tax-exempt charitable trusts are not required to file profits tax returns with the IRD. They are, however, required to keep accounting records (s. 51C(1)). Charitable trusts are also subject to periodic reviews by the IRD. Upon review, the trust will be asked to furnish, amongst other things, accounts and supplementary documents and information to ascertain whether the charity's objects are still charitable and its activities are compatible with its objects.

241. With respect to private express trusts that are not carrying on a business (including foreign trusts), the obligations on a trustee to maintain accounting records arise only from the requirements of common law. Under common law, trustees have a duty to keep clear and accurate accounts and produce them to any beneficiary when required.[32] A trustee must also provide to the beneficiaries accurate information of the disposition of the trust fund.[33] Hong Kong authorities report that trustees have a common law duty to keep records that: correctly explain the trust's transactions; enable the trust's financial position to be determined with reasonable accuracy at any

32. *Pearse v Green* (1819) 1 Jacob & Walker 135 at 140, Hotung v Ho Yuen Ki [2007] 4 HKLRD 384 and The Rules of the High Court Administration and Similar Actions – Order 85.
33. *Walker v Symonds* (1818) 36 E.R. 751.

time; allow financial statements to be prepared; and maintain underlying documentation such as invoices and contracts.

242. In summary, trustees of private express trusts and foreign trusts are statutorily required to maintain accounting records where the trust is carrying on business in Hong Kong. Moreover, where the trustee is subject to AML/CFT (financial institutions and lawyers), transactional records are required to be maintained.

243. The Hong Kong authorities report that trustees have a common law duty to keep accounting records.

244. It is noted that in relation to foreign trusts, which are governed by foreign law (including common law), it is conceivable that certain aspects of the common law may not be applied by the jurisdiction whose laws govern the trust or even that such jurisdiction may be a civil law one. In any event, even where the common law applies, the question remains whether there is sufficient oversight by a Hong Kong government authority on whether information or documents are being kept in all cases.

245. In practice, the Hong Kong authorities monitor Hong Kong trustees in relation to domestic or foreign trusts that carry on business in Hong Kong. Similarly, there is monitoring and supervision of the keeping of transactional records under AML. However, in cases which are subject only to common law requirements there is no systematic monitoring on whether resident trustees of private express trusts or foreign trusts in Hong Kong keep accounting records that meet the international standards. During the three-year period under review, Hong Kong did not receive any requests concerning accounting records of trusts. Hong Kong should monitor whether Hong Kong resident trustees keep accounting records that fully meet that international standards and that those records are kept for at least five years in all cases.

246. The management company of unit trusts and real estate investment trusts authorised by the Securities and Futures Commission are obliged to issue to holders and file with the commission annual reports and semi-annual reports of the trusts within four months of the year-end and two months of the period-end respectively. The Securities and Futures Commission has set out in the relevant product codes the content requirements of financial reports of unit trusts and real estate investment trusts. The annual reports must include *inter alia* the auditors' opinion on the financial statements of the trusts and the trustee's opinion on whether the management company has in all material respects managed trusts in accordance with the provisions of the constitutive documents.

247. Trustees of provident fund schemes must ensure that such accounting records are kept so as to correctly record and explain all transactions concerning the scheme and the financial position of the scheme (*Mandatory*

Provident Fund Schemes (General) Regulation s. 93). The trustee must also ensure that all records in respect of the management of the scheme (other than accounting records) are kept as will correctly record and explain the operation of the scheme (s. 92(1)).

248. For occupational retirement schemes, the trustee or administrator is obliged to keep proper accounts and records as regards all assets, liabilities and financial transactions of the scheme (*Occupational Retirement Schemes Ordinance* s. 20(1)). The accounts and records required to be kept include financial statements prepared in relation to a registered scheme which reflect a true and fair view of the financial transactions of the scheme during the year and of the disposition (s. 20).

Underlying documentation (ToR A.2.2)

249. All legal entities and arrangements that carry on a trade, profession, or business in Hong Kong (including foreign entities) have a statutory obligation to maintain underlying documentation (*Inland Revenue Ordinance* ss.51C(3) and (4)). Underlying documentation to be maintained includes vouchers, bank statements, invoices, receipts, and other documents necessary to verify the entries in the books of account (s. 51C). While contracts are not explicitly mentioned, all contracts that relate to accounting entries and are necessary to verify the entries in the books of account must be maintained.

250. Under s. 2(1A) of the *Business Registration Ordinance*, a company which is incorporated in Hong Kong or a non-Hong Kong company which is required to register in Hong Kong is deemed to be a person carrying on a business and liable for registration under the *Business Registration Ordinance*. Upon the coming into operation of the *Business Registration (Amendment) Ordinance 2010*, simultaneous application for company incorporation and business registration is mandatory and profits tax files are opened instantly for all companies registered with the Companies Registry. Accordingly, the requirements and obligations imposed under s. 51C(3)(b) of the *Inland Revenue Ordinance*, including the obligation to maintain underlying documentation, apply to all legal entities and arrangements incorporated/registered under the *Companies Ordinance/Business Registration Ordinance* regardless of whether they derive profits chargeable to tax in Hong Kong. In practice, the IRD periodically reviews the tax positions of companies or partnerships that do not derive profits chargeable to tax in Hong Kong. When these companies or partnerships are subject to an audit, they may need to provide underlying documentation to the IRD to evidence that their profits are indeed not subject to tax in Hong Kong. The IRD advises that IRD auditors need to check (and receive access to) underlying documentation before concluding a tax audit. Companies or partnerships that did not report taxable income are selected for in-depth examinations.

Document retention *(ToR A.2.3)*

251. The *Inland Revenue Ordinance* provides that the accounting records and underlying documentation must be maintained for a period of not less than seven years after the completion of the transactions, acts or operations to which they relate (s. 51C(1)).

252. The *Companies Ordinance* provides that any books of account which a company is required to prepare or maintain must be preserved for seven years from the end of the financial year to which the last entry made or matter recorded relates (s. 121). A person who was a director of a company immediately before its dissolution must ensure that all the books and papers of the company are kept for not less than five years after the dissolution (s. 292(3)).

253. The *Inland Revenue Ordinance* provides that partnerships are obliged to maintain accounting records for a period of not less than seven years after the completion of the transactions, acts or operations to which they relate (s. 51C(1)). The seven-year requirement also applies to dissolved partnerships.

254. If a trustee carries on a trade, profession or business in Hong Kong, it is required to maintain business records for a period of not less than seven years after the completion of the transactions, acts or operations to which they relate (*Inland Revenue Ordinance* s. 51C(1)). Licensed corporations (including management companies of a unit trust) are required to maintain accounting records for not less than seven years (*Securities and Futures (Keeping of Records) Rules* s. 3). Trustees of provident fund schemes are required to maintain accounting records for at least seven years after the end of the financial period in which the record was made or, if the record relates to a person's membership of the scheme, for at least 7 years after the person ceases to be a scheme member (*Mandatory Provident Fund Schemes (General) Regulation* s. 93).

Conclusion and practice

255. In conclusion, the legal and regulatory framework for ensuring the availability of accounting records and underlying documentation is in place in Hong Kong. Relevant entities are subject to the obligations under the *Inland Revenue Ordinance* and other ordinances specific to particular types of legal entities to keep reliable accounting records, including underlying documentation for a period of at least five years. All Hong Kong companies must keep accounts pursuant to the *Companies Ordinance* and those accounts must be audited. General and limited partnerships are entities carrying on business in Hong Kong and accordingly fall within the scope of the *Inland Revenue Ordinance*. Together, the tax and commercial obligations result in Hong Kong being able to provide accounting information to its EOI partners when requested.

256. Nonetheless, trustees of private express trusts and foreign trusts are only statutorily required to maintain accounting records where the trust is carrying on business in Hong Kong. It is also noted that, where the trustee is subject to AML/CFT, transactional records are required to be maintained by persons subject to AML (financial institutions and lawyers).Where a private express trust or foreign trust is not carrying on business in Hong Kong, there is no systematic monitoring by a Hong Kong government authority on whether accounting records or underlying documents are being maintained and whether they would fully meet the international standards.

257. The IRD has a wide range of instruments at its disposal to administer and enforce its tax base and ensure compliance with legal obligations. The Companies Registry also has instruments to enforce the legal obligations it administers. The IRD has an automated system to monitor the filing of tax returns. The failure to file tax returns is subject to penalties which are applied in practice (see statistics for the number of cases and amounts collected in section A.1.6 above). Moreover, returns are verified by IRD officers and penalties are applied when the submission of false or incorrect information is identified (see section A.1.6 above for penalties applied in practice). The IRD system allows for cross-checking of tax returns of different taxpayers as well as the identification of significant difference in the amount of assessable profits. Discrepancies identified would normally trigger audits. The Field Audit and Investigation Unit of the IRD investigates more than a thousand cases per year and keeps statistics on the number of cases completed, the understated earnings and profits, tax and penalties assessed and collected.

258. In order to reply to requests for accounting information, the first step taken by the IRD would be to review its database for filed tax returns and financial statements. The IRD can also access information directly from the taxpayer by serving a notice. These procedures would be followed in situations where accounting records or underlying documentation is requested by a treaty partner.

259. Hong Kong's EOI partners reported having requested accounting information during the period under review and that such information was provided in a timely manner. In one of the cases, the information requested related to authenticated copies of accounting books. Hong Kong has declined to reply to two requests made by a treaty partner on the basis of absence of a domestic tax interest (more details in parts B and C of this report), since the treaty with the relevant treaty partner did not contain a provision equivalent to article 26(4) of the OECD Model Convention. The information requested in those two cases included contracts and other business records. Hong Kong and that treaty partner have already signed a protocol containing a provision equivalent to article 26(4) of the OECD Model Convention and now Hong Kong is able to provide information in relation to which it has no domestic tax interest to this treaty partner.

Determination and factors underlying recommendations

Phase 1 determination	
The element is in place.	
Factors underlying recommendations	**Recommendations**
Trustees of private express trusts and foreign trusts are only statutorily required to maintain accounting records where the trust is carrying on business in Hong Kong.	Hong Kong should ensure that trustees of private express trusts and foreign trusts maintain accounting records even where the trust is not carrying on business in Hong Kong.

Phase 2 rating	
Largely Compliant	
Factors underlying recommendations	**Recommendations**
In circumstances where Hong Kong trustees of private express trusts or foreign trusts are not Hong Kong financial institutions or lawyers, and the trust neither carries on business in Hong Kong nor derives income which is taxable in Hong Kong, there is no systematic monitoring by government authorities of whether accounting records or underlying documents are being maintained.	Hong Kong should monitor whether Hong Kong resident trustees keep accounting records in all cases that fully meet the international standards and that those records are kept for at least five years.

A.3. Banking information

Banking information should be available for all account-holders.

260. Hong Kong maintains a three-tier system of deposit-taking institutions, namely, licensed banks, restricted licence banks and deposit-taking companies. They are collectively known as "authorised institutions" under the Banking Ordinance. Authorised institutions may operate in Hong Kong as either locally incorporated companies or branches of foreign banks. Authorised institutions are subject to the supervision of HKMA.

Record-keeping requirements (ToR A.3.1)

261. Authorised institutions are subject to CDD and record-keeping requirements stipulated in the *AMLO* as supplemented by the revised mandatory Bank Guidelines issued by the HKMA in July 2012. The *AMLO*

provides that authorised institutions are obliged to maintain account and transactional records and customer identity information obtained during the course of CDD procedures for at least six years following the closure of the account or following the completion of the transaction, as the case may be (Schedule 2 s. 20). In cases where the records relate to on-going investigations, or transactions which have been the subject of a disclosure, they must be retained until it is confirmed that the case has been closed (*AMLO Guidelines* paras. 8.4, 8.6).

262. The *AMLO* Guidelines also provide that authorised institutions should maintain information regarding: the identity of the parties to the transaction; the nature and date of the transaction; the type and amount of currency involved; the origin of the funds (if known); the form in which the funds were offered or withdrawn (e.g. cash, cheques, etc); the destination of the funds; the form of instruction and authority; and the type and identifying number of any account involved in the transaction (where applicable) (*AMLO Guidelines* para. 8.5).

263. Under Section 21 of the *AMLO*, the HKMA is empowered to impose a range of supervisory sanctions including publicly reprimanding the financial institution; ordering it to take any remedial action; imposing fines not exceeding the greater of *(i)* HKD 10 million (EUR 0.99 million) or *(ii)* three times the amount of profit gained, or costs avoided, by the financial institution as a result of the contravention. The HKMA has developed a programme of on-site and off-site examinations. In 2012, it conducted 19 examinations focusing on the authorised institutions' AML/CFT controls. There were 200 authorised institutions in 2012. Since the *AMLO* came into effect on 1 April 2012, the HKMA has not yet imposed sanctions on any authorised institutions for contravention of a specific provision under the *AMLO*, including the record-keeping requirements. However, the HKMA reports it takes failures in AML/CFT controls very seriously and will use the full range of powers available to it, both under *AMLO* and the *Banking Ordinance*, where the circumstances of the case warrant. No prosecutions have been conducted so far.

264. There are sufficient legal obligations in place for banks and other financial institutions to maintain all records pertaining to accounts as well as to related financial and transactional information in Hong Kong.

265. In order to access bank information, the Hong Kong authorities will usually issue a notice to produce to the relevant financial institution pursuant to sections 51(4)(a) and 51(4AA) of the Inland Revenue Ordinance, requiring the information to be provided within a prescribed time limit. Normally the time limit is 14 to 21 days, depending on the degree of accessibility of the information and the volume of documents involved. Failure to comply with the requirements of the notice will be subject to a fine of HKD 10 000 (EUR 987) and the court may order the person to furnish the required information within

a specified time. During the period under review, the IRD did not need to impose the sanctions provided under the Inland Revenue Ordinance, as all third-party information holders provided the information when requested by the tax authority.

266. Banking information was one of the categories of information Hong Kong was specifically requested to provide to its EOI partners. Information requested included bank account details, credit vouchers and remittance vouchers. There have been no instances where the requisite information was not provided to Hong Kong's EOI partners. Over the three-year period under review 14 requests were made for banking information, Hong Kong was able to provide banking information in all cases. Generally, this information was made available within 90 days.

Determination and factors underlying recommendations

Phase 1 determination
The element is in place.

Phase 2 rating
Compliant

B. Access to Information

Overview

267. A variety of information may be needed in a tax enquiry and jurisdictions should have the authority to obtain all such information. This includes information held by banks and other financial institutions as well as information concerning the ownership of companies or the identity of interest holders in other persons or entities, such as partnerships and trusts, as well as accounting information in respect of all such entities. This section of the report examines whether Hong Kong's legal and regulatory framework gives the authorities access powers that cover all relevant persons and information and whether rights and safeguards are compatible with effective exchange of information. It also assesses the effectiveness of this framework in practice.

268. Hong Kong's Inland Revenue Department (IRD) has extensive powers to obtain bank, ownership, identity, and accounting information and has measures to compel the production of such information. The ability of the IRD to obtain information for international EOI purposes is derived from its general access powers under the *Inland Revenue Ordinance* coupled with the authority provided by the relevant exchange of information agreements (ss.51 and 51B). Sections 51 and 51B were extended in 2010 to enable the IRD to access information in order to respond to international requests pursuant to DTCs signed by or amended by Hong Kong since passage of those amendments. Since 19 July 2013, Hong Kong law also allows information to be accessed in respect of an EOI request made under a TIEA.

269. In practice, Hong Kong's competent authority has been able to gather information from taxpayers or third parties to respond to EOI requests. The Hong Kong authorities issue a formal notice to gather information in such cases. As a general rule, the Hong Kong authorities are required to notify the person that is the subject of the request. Hong Kong can waive the notification requirement and has done so in practice in a number of cases where such a notification would likely undermine the prospects of success of the investigation conducted by its EOI partners.

270. The IRD also has the power to search premises and seize information and to obtain compelled testimony. To date, the Hong Kong authorities have not had to impose sanctions or employ search and seizure measures to compel the production of information in relation to an EOI request. There are no statutory bank secrecy provisions in place that would restrict effective EOI. Hong Kong had no difficulties accessing bank information in response to an EOI request during the period under review.

271. The rights or safeguards (e.g. notification, appeal rights) in Hong Kong do not appear to restrict or delay effective EOI. The definition of information subject to legal privilege that cannot be disclosed under a prescribed EOI request is limited to communications made in connection with the giving of legal advice to a client or in connection with judicial proceedings. To date, there have been no instances in which attorney-client privilege has been invoked by persons from whom information has been requested. In practice, the rights and safeguards that apply in Hong Kong have not restricted or delayed an answer to an EOI request.

B.1. Competent Authority's ability to obtain and provide information

Competent authorities should have the power to obtain and provide information that is the subject of a request under an exchange of information arrangement from any person within their territorial jurisdiction who is in possession or control of such information (irrespective of any legal obligation on such person to maintain the secrecy of the information).

272. The Commissioner of Inland Revenue or his authorised representative is the competent authority of Hong Kong. The competent authority is empowered by the Inland Revenue Ordinance to obtain full information, including ownership, identity, accounting or banking information for purposes of responding to an EOI request. The Commissioner has authorised his two Deputy Commissioners as the authorised representatives. The Deputy Commissioner of Inland Revenue (Technical) also oversees the Tax Treaty Section which is responsible for all matters relating to international tax, including EOI with treaty partners.

273. The IRD has 2 818 employees, of which 1 852 perform duties directly concerned with taxation. Other employees provide administrative, information technology and clerical support services. The IRD is mainly organised in specific units which are allocated responsibilities for a certain tax or with a broader auditing function. In addition to the Tax Treaty Section, other units within the IRD (Unit 1 – Profits Tax, Unit 2 – Individuals Tax, Unit 4 – Investigations and the Headquarters Unit – Property Tax) are also involved in information gathering and preparation of responses to EOI requests. The Hong Kong authorities report that all IRD officers dealing with EOI

matters have minimum tertiary qualifications of a bachelor degree in related fields and/or professional qualifications in accounting as well as more than 10 years' experience in tax administration.

Bank, ownership, and identity information (ToR B.1.1) and accounting records (ToR B.1.2)

274. The IRD has access to databases in which ownership, identity and accounting information collected by the IRD itself, by the Companies Registry or the Land Registry is maintained. The Hong Kong competent authority is, therefore, able to reply to a number of requests without having to make requests to external parties. However, when requests cover, for instance, business records, accounting books, underlying documentation or banking information, the Hong Kong authorities need to contact the information holder.

275. The IRD's powers to access information are contained in the *Inland Revenue Ordinance* (ss.51 and 51B). Originally, these powers contemplated obtaining information whenever Hong Kong had a domestic interest in the matter. However, in 2010 they were extended to enable the IRD to access information for EOI purposes pursuant to a DTC. Specifically, the *Inland Revenue (Amendment) Ordinance* 2010, effective 12 March 2010, extends the IRD's access powers "for the purposes of obtaining full information in regard to any matter that may affect the tax liability, responsibility, or obligation of any person under the laws of a territory outside Hong Kong concerning any tax of that territory" pursuant to a request made under a DTC (ss.5, 6 and 7). Since 19 July 2013, with the enactment of the *Inland Revenue (Amendment) (No. 2) Ordinance 2013*, the IRD's powers have been extended to cover access to information in response to requests made under any arrangements for the exchange of information, including TIEAs.

276. The IRD may give notice in writing asking any person (including banks and other financial institutions) to furnish all information, including any deeds, plans, instruments, books, accounts, trade lists stock lists, vouchers, bank statements or any other relevant document, in his or her possession in regard to any matter that may affect any liability, responsibility or obligation of any person under the *Inland Revenue Ordinance* (s. 51(4)(a)). The *Inland Revenue (Amendment) (No. 2) Ordinance 2013* also clarified that the IRD's access powers extend to information that is under a person's control, in addition to information that is in a person's possession. The IRD may give notice in writing to such person or third party requiring him or her to attend and be examined, and upon such examination to answer truthfully all questions put to him or her respecting any such matter (s. 51(4)(b)). These powers also apply for the purposes of obtaining full information in response to an international EOI request made pursuant to a DTC (s. 51(4AA)). As mentioned

above, since 19 July 2013, these powers also apply in connection to a TIEA (the *Inland Revenue (Amendment) (No. 2) Ordinance 2013*).

277. The Commissioner of Inland Revenue or an IRD officer not below the rank of chief assessor can obtain a search warrant from a magistrate authorising the Commissioner or the authorised officer to search, take possession of, and retain any books, records or documents of any person (s. 51B). This provision applies to tax of a foreign territory for the purpose of exchange of information under a DTC (s. 51B(1AA)). Since 19 July 2013, these powers also apply in connection to a TIEA (the *Inland Revenue (Amendment) (No. 2) Ordinance 2013*).

278. There are no legal or procedural limitations on how a person may be reviewed or audited or the number of times they may be reviewed or audited that would limit the ability of Hong Kong's competent authority or field staff to use their access powers for the purpose of EOI requests.

279. The Schedule to the *Inland Revenue (Disclosure of Information) Rules* (the *Disclosure Rules*) (as amended by the *Inland Revenue (Amendment) (No. 2) Ordinance 2013)*, which is part of the legal framework in Hong Kong for EOI, sets forth the information to be contained in a request for information pursuant to a DTC or a TIEA (which can be waived; see further below):

- the identity of the person or authority that makes the disclosure request;
- the purpose of the disclosure request;
- the identity of the person who is the subject of the disclosure request[34];
- a statement on the information requested, including: (a) the nature of the information; (b) the relevance of the information; and (c) the form in which the competent authority wishes to receive the information;
- the ground for believing that the information requested is held by Hong Kong's Commissioner of Inland Revenue or is in the possession or control of a person in Hong Kong;
- the name and address of any person believed to have possession or control of the information requested;
- a statement that: (a) the disclosure request complies with the laws and administrative practices of the requesting government's territory; (b) the competent authority is able to obtain the information under the laws of the requesting government's territory or in the normal course of the administrative practices of the requesting government's territory; and (c) the disclosure request complies with the relevant arrangements;

34. See Art. 5(5)(a) of the OECD *Model TIEA*.

- a statement that the requesting government has pursued all means available in its territory to obtain the information, including getting the information directly from the person who is the subject of the disclosure request;
- the tax period for which information is requested;
- the period within which the competent authority wishes the disclosure request to be met;
- if applicable, a statement: (a) confirming that the competent authority is of the opinion that notification to the person who is the subject of the disclosure request is likely to undermine the chance of success of the investigation in relation to which the request is made; and (b) giving reasons for the opinion; and
- if applicable, a statement: (a) confirming that the competent authority is of the opinion that prior notification to the person who is the subject of the disclosure request is likely to frustrate the timely enforcement of the tax laws of the requesting government's territory; and (b) giving reasons for the opinion.

280. The *Disclosure Rules* empower the Commissioner of Inland Revenue, on reasonable grounds, to approve a disclosure request even if the request does not contain the particulars set out in the Schedule (s. 3(2)(b)). There is no list of what constitutes "reasonable grounds". The IRD's administrative guidance[35] provides that whether departure would be permitted would be decided by the particular circumstances of each case. As a bare minimum, the Commissioner would require the following particulars to be provided in the request: the identity of the subject person; the purpose of the request and the relevance of the information to such purpose (i.e. the "foreseeably relevant" requirement); and the nature of the information required. Hong Kong's IRD has confirmed that the requirement to provide the name and address of any person believed to have possession or control of the information requested will be waived if the information is not known. The IRD reports that this waiver has been exercised in practice. In such cases, the IRD will access the information from the person(s) who it believes is in possession or control of the information. Moreover, Hong Kong could also waive, for instance, the requirement that the requesting jurisdiction approach the person who is the subject of the disclosure request to get the information. In practice, the Hong Kong authorities confirmed that they would only expect that requesting jurisdiction follows the guidance provided in the Commentary to Article 26 of the OECD Model Convention, which provides in paragraph 9(a) that requesting

35. Departmental Interpretation and Practice Note No. 47, *Exchange of Information under Comprehensive Double Taxation Agreements.*

jurisdictions should rely upon "the regular sources of information available under the internal taxation procedure" before sending an EOI request to a foreign jurisdiction.

281. Since 19 July 2013, Hong Kong's legal framework for accessing and exchanging information pursuant to a TIEA is in place. As a result, Hong Kong's competent authority has power to obtain and provide to requesting jurisdictions relevant information held by banks, other financial institutions, and any person with a statutory secrecy obligation under a TIEA as well. So far, however, Hong Kong has not concluded any TIEAs. The Hong Kong authorities report that they have been in contact with a number of jurisdictions and anticipate being able to start formal negotiations soon.

Bank information

282. There are no limitations on the ability of Hong Kong's IRD to access bank account information maintained by banks or other financial institutions. Under the *Inland Revenue Ordinance*, the IRD has the power to obtain information held by a bank or other financial institution for either civil or criminal tax purposes in response to a specific EOI request for such information (s. 51(4)). Hong Kong has no bank secrecy laws. The information gathering procedures are the same for a bank, a service provider or a person that is the subject of the enquiry. To gather information from these parties, the officer in charge will issue a notice to the information holder requiring the information to be provided within a prescribed time limit. Normally the time limit is around 14 to 21 days, depending on the degree of accessibility of the information and the volume of documents involved.

283. For the purposes of obtaining bank information, the IRD normally requires the requesting party to specify the name of the account holder and his or her identification number (such as Hong Kong Identity Card number, passport number or business registration number). In cases where the specified information is not available, other information (e.g. bank account number or similar identifying information) would then be needed. The Hong Kong authorities report that during the period under review there have been no cases where bank information was obtained when identifying information other than the name was provided. The Hong Kong authorities also report that they could in practice obtain bank information by using other identifying information such as bank account number, Hong Kong Identity Card number, passport number or Hong Kong Business Registration number. With regard to a disclosure request in which only the account number is provided, Hong Kong IRD has indicated that the absence of the name of the account holder would not be a hurdle, provided that a unique key identifying the account owner together with other supporting information and statements (as detailed in the OECD *Model TIEA* Art. 5 para. 5(b) to (g)) are furnished by the requesting jurisdiction.

Ownership and identity information and accounting records

284. There are no limitations on the ability of the IRD to access ownership and identity information and accounting records from taxpayers or third parties for civil or criminal tax purposes. There is no need for court approval when IRD officials request information from taxpayers or third parties. Court approval is required, however, to exercise search and seizure pursuant to the *Inland Revenue Ordinance* for either civil and criminal tax matters in the requesting jurisdiction.

285. The *Inland Revenue Ordinance* empowers the IRD to give notice in writing to any person whom it considers may be in possession of the necessary information and to require him or her to furnish all relevant information in his or her possession. Thus, where a person is not statutorily required to maintain the information but is in possession of such information, the IRD is empowered to access such information. Additionally, the IRD has the power to obtain information held by any person acting in an agency or fiduciary capacity, including nominees and trustees (s. 51(4)).

Use of access powers in practice

286. During the period under review, Hong Kong gathered a wide range of information to reply to requests made by its EOI partners. The information accessed includes banking information, beneficial ownership information (for the application of treaty benefits), information on employment income, ownership information, accounting information and supporting documentation, business records and tax returns.

287. The procedures for processing and gathering information for EOI requests are set out in written guidelines, circulars and handbooks developed by the IRD. Responsibilities for handling all steps of the information gathering process are clearly assigned. All incoming EOI requests are received by the Tax Treaty Section of the IRD. The officers in the Tax Treaty Section assess the validity of a request against the treaty and the *Disclosure Rules* and submit the case to the Deputy Commissioner of Inland Revenue for endorsement. After approval, the case is passed to the relevant IRD unit for handling. All information gathering, investigation and examinations are handled by the IRD units according to their specific competencies (and not the Tax Treaty section).

288. Where information needed to respond to a request is in the hands of the IRD, the case officer in charge is expected to access such information expeditiously and prepare a draft reply in a short time frame (approximately 30 days from the receipt of the request). In cases where information is held by another government department, a notice pursuant to s. 52(1) of the *Inland Revenue Ordinance* is issued. Co-operation from other department is also expected within a short time frame and the case officer in charge is also expected to draft a reply within approximately 30 days.

289. Where it is necessary to gather information held by external parties (such as a bank, a service provider or the person that is the subject of the enquiry), the case officer in charge issues a notice to the information holder requiring the information to be provided within a prescribed time limit. Normally the time limit is around 14 to 21 days, depending on the degree of accessibility of the information and the volume of documents involved. After receiving the information from the holder, the case officer prepares a draft reply to the request and provides it to the officer in charge in the Tax Treaty Section.

290. The Hong Kong authorities report that generally they have not encountered practical difficulties in obtaining information for EOI purposes. However, they have occasionally not received the full information requested and/or they have not received an answer within the agreed time limit. In those circumstances, the case officer has proactively followed up with the information holder to obtain the full information requested. No sanctions were needed to be applied to obtain information during the period under review. During the period under review, there was no instance where Hong Kong was not able to access information.

291. However, there was one aspect of Hong Kong's EOI framework in place during the period under review that could have restricted its ability to provide information to its EOI partners. Hong Kong's old framework prevented the exchange of any information that preceded the effective date of the EOI agreement, notwithstanding that it was relevant to a period after the EOI agreement came into effect (see *section C.1.9* of this report). However, since 19 July 2013, following the enactment of the *Inland Revenue (Amendment) (No. 2) Ordinance 2013*, the Commissioner of Inland Revenue is able to exchange information relating to the administration or enforcement of the tax law of an EOI partner in respect of any period that starts after the EOI arrangement came into operation, even if the information pre-dates such period. This applies to both DTCs and TIEAs.

Use of information gathering measures absent domestic tax interest (ToR B.1.3)

292. The concept of "domestic tax interest" describes a situation where a contracting party can only provide information to another contracting party if it has an interest in the requested information for its own tax purposes. Hong Kong has no domestic tax interest with respect to its information gathering powers for purposes of international exchange of information pursuant to its DTCs signed subsequent to the enactment of the *Inland Revenue (Amendment) Ordinance* 2010. Similar provisions apply to TIEAs under the *Inland Revenue (Amendment) (No. 2) Ordinance 2013*. Information gathering powers provided to Hong Kong's tax authorities under the *Inland Revenue Ordinance* can be used to provide EOI assistance regardless of whether Hong Kong needs the information for its own domestic tax purposes (s. 51AA).

293. Three of Hong Kong's 29 DTCs (with Belgium, Thailand, and Vietnam) were signed prior to the enactment of the *Inland Revenue (Amendment) Ordinance* 2010. As a result of the manner Hong Kong has removed its domestic tax interest, Hong Kong is required to enter into protocols (or new DTCs) to bring these three DTCs to the international standard. Until it is able to do so, the IRD can therefore exercise its information gathering powers for EOI purposes under these DTCs only to the extent that it has a domestic tax interest. Hong Kong's competent authority reports that it has contacted Belgium, Thailand, and Vietnam on a number of occasions in order to update the respective DTCs in line with the standard. It is recommended that Hong Kong continue its efforts to update these agreements to ensure that its competent authority has the power to obtain all relevant information with respect to all of its EOI partners. The Hong Kong authorities report that, in June 2013, they received Vietnam's consent to update the EOI article in line with the standard and are arranging for the signing of a protocol to upgrade the EOI article. The Hong Kong authorities received feedback from the Belgian tax administration on the proposed upgrade to the EOI provision of their DTC in early August 2013. The Hong Kong authorities report that they are actively following this up with the Belgian authorities. In relation to Thailand, Hong Kong has contacted with the Thai competent authorities to update the EOI article in line with the international standard since 2010. However, a reply from Thailand in this regard is still pending.

294. During the period under review and prior to the 2010 amendment abolishing Hong Kong's domestic tax interest requirement, Hong Kong received two information requests pursuant to a treaty that did not comply with the standard with regard to domestic tax interest. Owing to the limitation in its information gathering powers at that time, the IRD was unable to reply to the requests as they concerned information in which the IRD had no domestic interest. It is noted that a protocol was subsequently signed with the treaty partner in question, which contains a provision akin to Article 26(4) of the OECD. As such, Hong Kong is now in a position to gather information upon the request of such treaty partner regardless of a domestic tax interest.

Compulsory powers *(ToR B.1.4)*

295. As previously described, Hong Kong's tax authorities have broad powers to compel the production of information from natural and legal persons. Under the *Inland Revenue Ordinance*, the IRD has powers of discovery and inspection, and is able to compel production of any documents deemed relevant to their examination from taxpayers and third party record keepers (ss.51 and 51B). The IRD also has the power to compel testimony from taxpayers and third parties (s. 51).

296. The Commissioner of Inland Revenue or an IRD officer not below the rank of chief assessor can obtain a search warrant from a magistrate

authorising the Commissioner or the authorised officer to search, take possession of, and retain any books, records or documents of any person (s. 51B). This provision applies to tax of a foreign territory for the purpose of exchange of information under a DTC (s. 51B(1AA)). Since 19 July 2013, this provision also applies for the purpose of exchange of information under a TIEA (the *Inland Revenue (Amendment) (No. 2) Ordinance 2013*, s. 6).

297. Any person who without reasonable excuse fails to comply with the requirements of a notice given to him or her under section 51(4)(a) or fails to attend in answer to a notice issued under section 51(4)(b) or, having attended, fails to answer any questions put to him or her is liable to a civil penalty at level three (HKD 10 000) (EUR 987) and a court may order the person to furnish the required information within a time specified in the court order. The same penalties apply whether the information is sought for domestic or foreign tax purposes (s. 51(4AA)). Additionally, any person who obstructs or hinders the Commissioner of Inland Revenue or an authorised officer acting in the discharge of his or her duties under s. 51B (search and seizure) commits an offence and is liable on conviction to a fine at level three (HKD 10 000) and to imprisonment for six months (s. 51B(4)).

298. During the period under review, the IRD did not need to impose the sanctions provided under the *Inland Revenue Ordinance*, as all third-party information holders provided the information when requested by the tax authority. On some occasions, a follow-up on the original request was necessary; however, no sanctions were imposed in those cases because information was provided promptly.

Secrecy provisions *(ToR B.1.5)*

299. There are no provisions under Hong Kong's laws relating to the secrecy of ownership, identity or accounting information. The *Inland Revenue Ordinance* overrides confidentiality provisions applicable to banks and other financial institutions in Hong Kong (s. 51).

300. The *Inland Revenue Ordinance* provides that except in the performance of his or her duties under the *Inland Revenue Ordinance*, officers of the IRD are obliged to preserve and aid in preserving secrecy with regard to all matters relating to the affairs of any taxpayer coming to their knowledge (s. 4). However, where any EOI agreements have effect, this secrecy obligation does not prevent the disclosure of requested information to any authorised officer of the contracting party (s. 49(5)). Therefore, disclosure of information to treaty partners under the relevant exchange of information provisions in Hong Kong's EOI agreements does not contravene the secrecy provisions under the *Inland Revenue Ordinance*.

Professional secrecy

301. All of Hong Kong's EOI agreements permit Hong Kong to decline a request if responding to it would disclose any trade, business, industrial, commercial or professional secret or trade process, or information, the disclosure of which would be contrary to public policy. This follows the international standard.

302. Among the situations in which Hong Kong is not obliged to supply information in response to a request is when the requested information would disclose communications protected by attorney-client privilege. The scope of attorney client privilege is not defined in statute. At common law, the privilege attaches to confidential written or oral communications between a professional legal adviser and his client, or any person representing the client, in connection with and in contemplation of, and for the purposes of legal proceedings or in connection with the giving of legal advice.[36] The privilege applies to communications between a legal adviser (i.e. barristers, solicitors) and the client. It does not apply to communications between the client and third parties (for which no attorney-client relationship exists). Where an attorney acts in any other capacity other than as an attorney (e.g. as a nominee shareholder, a trustee, a company director or under a power of attorney), the attorney-client privilege does not apply.[37] In this case, EOI resulting from and relating to any such communications cannot be declined because of attorney-client privilege. The attorney-client privilege is confined to the legal profession. There is no other professional privilege besides the attorney-client privilege. For example, the privilege does not extend to communications between a person and his medical adviser[38] or with his accountant[39].

303. According to Hong Kong's EOI partners, to date there have been no instances where a request for information was not answered because of secrecy provisions. The competent authority has also confirmed that it has not encountered difficulties in accessing information held by third parties such as attorneys, accountants or other professionals.

36. Wilson v Rastall [1792] 4 Term Rep 753; Minter v Priest [1930] AC 558.
37. The attorney-client privilege does not apply to communication if it is made for the purpose of, or as part of the process of, crime, fraud, abuse of statutory power or for the purpose of stifling or covering up a crime or fraud or in some circumstances defeating or frustrating the administration of justice by the court or when both are engaged in the commission of some wrongful act (China Light and Power Co Ltd v Ford [1998] 1 HKLRD 382 CA).
38. C v. C [1946] 1 All ER 562.
39. R (Prudential) v. Special Commissioner of Income Tax (2010) EWCA Civ 1094.

Determination and factors underlying recommendations

Phase 1 determination	
The element is in place.	
Factors underlying recommendations	**Recommendations**
Hong Kong has a domestic tax interest requirement with respect to 3 of its 29 exchange of information partners. Hong Kong's competent authority has contacted the relevant exchange of information partners on a number of occasions to update the respective EOI provisions in line with the standard.	Hong Kong should continue its efforts to ensure that its competent authority has the power to obtain all relevant information with respect to all exchange of information agreements (regardless of their form).

Phase 2 rating
Compliant

B.2. Notification requirements and rights and safeguards

The rights and safeguards (e.g. notification, appeal rights) that apply to persons in the requested jurisdiction should be compatible with effective exchange of information.

Not unduly prevent or delay exchange of information (ToR B.2.1)

304. The *Terms of Reference* provides that rights and safeguards should not unduly prevent or delay effective exchange of information. For instance, notification rules should permit exceptions from prior notification (e.g. in cases in which the information request is of a very urgent nature or the notification is likely to undermine the chance of success of the investigation conducted by the requesting jurisdiction).

305. In Hong Kong, notification and review mechanisms are provided under the *Inland Revenue (Disclosure of Information) Rules* (the *Disclosure Rules*). Hong Kong's competent authority is obliged, subject to specified exceptions, to notify the person who is the subject of the request prior to providing the information to the requesting jurisdiction (s. 5). The person may request the information to be amended on the grounds that the information does not relate to him or her (e.g. the information relates to the wrong person), or that the information or part thereof is factually incorrect (s. 5(3)). Such requests must be made within 21 days after he or she has received a copy of the information from the Commissioner of Inland Revenue. The

Commissioner of Inland Revenue may, on the basis of the factual evidence available, accede to the request for amendment in full or partially or refuse the request.

306. In practice, the Hong Kong authorities inform their EOI partners about the rights and safeguards applicable in Hong Kong, including the notification rules. This allows partners to request a waiver of (prior) notification in their EOI requests, where they consider necessary (please see more details on the conditions for the waiver later in this section). The Hong Kong authorities are of the view that their notification and review mechanisms enhance the accuracy and integrity of the information to be exchanged, as the subject of the request is given an opportunity to amend any information that is factually incorrect.

307. The notification concerning the receipt of an EOI request is sent to the person that is the subject of the foreign request (the "*subject person*"). For instance, a request may be made by a foreign jurisdiction to gather information about a legal entity in Hong Kong that the foreign jurisdiction believes may be owned by one of its taxpayers, an individual. In these circumstances, Hong Kong would ordinarily send a notification to the Hong Kong company, which is the subject of the foreign enquiry, and not to the individual (the foreign taxpayer). In cases where, for instance, bank information is requested relating to transactions conducted by a Hong Kong company, the notification would be sent to the Hong Kong company, while the notice to produce the information or documents would normally be sent to the bank (unless, for instance, the requesting jurisdiction for any reason requests the Hong Kong authorities to request bank information to the subject person, a service provider etc.).

308. The Hong Kong authorities have developed a notification template to assist case officers and ensure that all notifications issued meet their departmental standards. The notification generally includes the following information: *(i)* a reference to the requesting jurisdiction; *(ii)* a reference to the EOI instrument under which the request is made; and *(iii)* a description of the information being requested. There is no legal requirement in Hong Kong concerning the need of the notification disclose for instance the name of the requesting jurisdiction or a reference to the EOI instrument under which the request is made.

309. The subject person has 14 days to request a copy of the information that the Commissioner of Inland Revenue intends to disclose to the requesting jurisdiction. The Hong Kong authorities report that the subject person will never receive a copy of the EOI request. The Hong Kong officials report that, in most cases, upon receiving the notification, the subject person asks for a copy of the information Hong Kong proposes to disclose. There have been no instances to date where the subject person has sought to amend the

information. On one occasion, in relation to a request for accounting records, the subject person inquired where the Hong Kong authorities had obtained the information. The authorities explained to the subject person that the accounting records in question were those filed by the subject person with its tax return. After receiving this clarification, the subject person made no further inquiries or objection to the disclosure of the information.

310. With regard to the details included in the notices to produce information, please refer to *section C.3* of this report. If the subject person is also requested to produce information, the subject person will receive both a notification and a notice to produce information at the same time. The Hong Kong authorities explained that the notification and the notice to produce information serve different purposes. They also explained that the notification as a general rule remains necessary as in many instances the IRD will be collecting information from different sources in order to reply to an EOI request. The notification, accordingly, provides an opportunity to the subject person to confirm that the information gathered is factually correct and relevant to the subject person.

311. The *Disclosure Rules* provide for a two-tier review: first by the Commissioner of Inland Revenue and then by the Financial Secretary. If the Commissioner refuses the request of the subject person to amend any part of the information that the Commissioner is prepared to disclose, that person may, by giving a notice in writing within 14 days after the Commissioner's notice of decision, request the Financial Secretary to review the Commissioner's decision. The Financial Secretary may approve, either in full or partially, or refuse the request. A written decision together with the reasons therefor will be given to the subject person. The decision of the Financial Secretary is final (s. 6).

312. As mentioned above, to date there have been no instances where the subject person has requested the amendment of information. Therefore, the second-tier of the process has not arisen in practice.

313. The competent authority is not required to notify the subject person if the competent authority has reasonable grounds to believe that (s. 5):

- all the addresses of the subject person known to the competent authority are undeliverable;
- notification is likely to undermine the chance of success of the investigation in relation to which the request is made; or
- the competent authority is under a tight time constraint to disclose the information in response to the request, such that: it is not practicable for the prior notification to be given, and the subsequent requests that the subject person may make in relation to the

information to be finally determined under the *Disclosure Rules*, within the time constraint; and the failure of the competent authority in disclosing the information to the requesting government within the time constraint is likely to frustrate the efforts of the requesting government in enforcing the tax laws of its territory.

314. In respect of urgent requests, the Departmental Interpretation and Practice Notes No. 47 of June 2010 provide the following guidance: the Hong Kong competent authority *must be satisfied that the urgency is genuine, for example, the information is required before a certain date because there is an imminent statutory time limit for raising the relevant tax assessment. However, this is not to be abused if the "urgency" is simply a result of deliberate or undue delay in making a request* (para. 64). The Hong Kong authorities report that Hong Kong has received one request in which the treaty partner asked for urgent provision of the information requested without stating any reason. In its request, the treaty partner also confirmed that prior notification would not frustrate the timely enforcement of its tax laws. The Hong Kong authorities sought to understand from the treaty partner the reason for the urgency, while simultaneously proceeding with gathering the requested information. The Hong Kong competent authority was satisfied with the reason provided by the treaty partner and agreed to dispense with prior notification. The notification was sent at the time when Hong Kong released the information to the treaty partner pursuant to section 8 of the Disclosure Rules

315. These reasonable grounds are based on information received from the requesting jurisdiction. The Schedule to the *Disclosure Rules* specifically provides that, amongst other information to be provided in a request for information under a DTC or a TIEA, the requesting jurisdiction may provide, if applicable:

- a statement: (a) confirming that the competent authority is of the opinion that notification to the person who is the subject of the disclosure request is likely to undermine the chance of success of the investigation in relation to which the request is made; and (b) giving reasons for the opinion; and
- a statement: (a) confirming that the competent authority is of the opinion that prior notification to the person who is the subject of the disclosure request is likely to frustrate the timely enforcement of the tax laws of the requesting government's territory; and (b) giving reasons for the opinion.

316. In practice, Hong Kong has waived the notification in relation to 15 requests where the foreign treaty partner confirmed that such notification would likely undermine the prospects of success of the investigation. It is

noted that the Hong Kong competent authority, when reviewing the facts and circumstances of the request, has on many occasions proactively inquired of Hong Kong's EOI partners whether they wished to request a waiver of notification (e.g. in criminal cases or cases where the foreign authority requested Hong Kong to obtain a search warrant).

317. If the competent authority is not obliged to provide prior notification to the subject person on the basis that it is under a tight time constraint to disclose the information in response to the requesting jurisdiction, notification must be made at the time when the information is disclosed to the requesting jurisdiction (*Disclosure Rules* s. 8). The notification must be in writing and notify the subject person of the nature of the information requested and that the subject person may request a copy of the information that the competent authority has disclosed to the requesting jurisdiction (s8). The two-tier review procedures set out earlier in this section will continue to apply in this case. In this case, if the review procedure results in any correction to the information already exchanged with the foreign competent authority, the Hong Kong competent authority will inform foreign competent authority accordingly and exchange the additional relevant information.

318. The peer input received for this review confirms that there have not been any situations where rights and safeguards that apply to a person in Hong Kong unduly prevented or delayed effective EOI.

Determination and factors underlying recommendations

Phase 1 determination
The element is in place.

Phase 2 rating
Compliant

C. Exchanging Information

Overview

319. Jurisdictions generally cannot exchange information for tax purposes unless they have a legal basis or mechanism for doing so. In Hong Kong, the legal authority to exchange information is derived from its exchange of information agreements as well as from domestic law. This section of the report examines whether Hong Kong's network of information exchange agreements meet the standard and whether its institutional framework is adequate to achieve effective exchange of information in practice.

320. Following Hong Kong's commitment to the internationally agreed standard for exchange of information for tax purposes in 2005, Hong Kong amended its tax legislation in 2010 to enable its competent authority to access information for EOI purposes without a domestic tax interest. Following this legislative amendment, Hong Kong has actively sought to extend its EOI network, signing 16 agreements or protocols incorporating the internationally agreed standard for EOI, of which 6 were in force by August 2010. In the last two years, it has rapidly expanded its network of EOI instruments and brought signed agreements into force. Hong Kong has signed in total 26 agreements that provide for effective EOI in tax matters in accordance with the international standard, of which 22 are in force.

321. All Hong Kong's agreements signed after its endorsement of the international standard contain the current version of Article 26 of the OECD *Model Taxation Convention*. Three of Hong Kong's agreements were signed prior to the legislative amendments in 2010 (with Belgium, Thailand and Vietnam) and EOI under these agreements remains subject to Hong Kong having a domestic tax interest. Hong Kong's competent authority reports that it has been in contact with these jurisdictions on a number of occasions to update the agreements in line with the standard. Hong Kong has no observations or reservations in respect of Article 26. The Hong Kong authorities report that, in June 2013, they received Vietnam's consent to update the EOI article in line with the standard and are arranging for the signing of a protocol to upgrade the EOI article. The Hong Kong authorities received feedback

from the Belgian tax administration on the proposed upgrade to the EOI provision of their DTC in early August 2013. The Hong Kong authorities report that they are actively following this up with the Belgian authorities. In relation to Thailand, Hong Kong has contacted with the Thai competent authorities to update the EOI article in line with the international standard since 2010. However, a reply from Thailand in this regard is still pending.

322. Hong Kong has signed agreements to the standard with 8 of its major trading partners, including with the PRC – Hong Kong's largest trading partner. A number of the Global Forum members have indicated that they have approached Hong Kong expressing interest in negotiating a TIEA without success as Hong Kong did not have a TIEA framework at the time and counter-proposed that a DTC be entered into. Since 19 July 2013, Hong Kong law allows for TIEAs and the Hong Kong authorities advise that Hong Kong is now in a position to enter into TIEAs with relevant partners. It is recommended that Hong Kong bring its existing agreements that do not meet the standard up to the standard and enter into agreements with all relevant EOI partners expeditiously.

323. All EOI articles in Hong Kong's agreements contain appropriate confidentiality provisions and Hong Kong's domestic legislation also contains relevant confidentiality provisions. These provisions apply equally to all information and documentation forming the requests received by Hong Kong as well as to responses received from counterparties.

324. Hong Kong's agreements ensure that the contracting parties are not obliged to provide information which would disclose trade, business, industrial, commercial or professional secrets or information which is the subject of attorney client privilege or to make disclosures which would be contrary to public policy. No concerns relating to these matters have been raised in practice.

325. During the period under review, there was one aspect of Hong Kong's EOI framework that restricted its ability to provide information to its EOI partners. Hong Kong's interpretation of its EOI agreements prevented the exchange of any information that preceded the effective date of the EOI agreement, notwithstanding that it was relevant to a period after the agreement came into effect. Hong Kong has amended its legislation to ensure that information that precedes the effective date of the agreement can be exchanged, provided that such information relates to a taxable period subsequent to the effective date of the EOI agreement.

326. Hong Kong has gained practical experience with exchanging information in recent years. Many processes and procedures were developed during the years coinciding with the period under review (1 July 2009 to 30 June 2012). Most requests received to date come from Hong Kong's main trading partner. Given the entry into force of a number of EOI agreements and

the continuous expansion of Hong Kong's EOI network in recent years, the number of incoming EOI requests can be expected to increase significantly.

327. Hong Kong's competent authority is well prepared to deal with increasing demand and has adequate resources to exchange information effectively. There is sufficient professional staff with clear responsibility for processing requests and retrieving and obtaining the requested information. The staff members also possess the requisite expertise and have undergone training specific to international EOI. Comprehensive guidelines have been issued covering all relevant steps of the EOI process.

328. The Hong Kong authorities have not yet made any outgoing EOI requests. However, detailed procedures and guidelines concerning the drafting and sending of such requests have been developed by the IRD.

329. In summary, Hong Kong has developed a sound system to exchange information. Feedback received from Hong Kong's peers confirms that Hong Kong's practices in connection with EOI are adequate, and they consider Hong Kong to be an efficient and co-operative EOI partner. The peers also acknowledged the great progress that Hong Kong has made in the last three years. Out of 61 incoming requests received during the period under review, Hong Kong answered 51 requests within 90 days, 8 from 91 to 180 days. Two cases took more than one year for Hong Kong to furnish a reply.

C.1. Exchange-of-information mechanisms

Exchange of information mechanisms should allow for effective exchange of information.

330. Hong Kong is signatory to EOI agreements with 29 jurisdictions – Austria, Belgium, Brunei, Canada, the PRC, the Czech Republic, France, Guernsey, Hungary, Indonesia, Ireland, Italy, Japan, Jersey, Kuwait, Liechtenstein, Luxembourg, Malaysia, Malta, Mexico, the Netherlands, New Zealand, Portugal, Qatar, Spain, Switzerland, Thailand, the United Kingdom and Vietnam. All those EOI agreements are DTCs.

331. Under all Hong Kong's EOI agreements, the Commissioner of Inland Revenue or his authorised representative is the competent authority of Hong Kong. After an EOI agreement has come into force, the Hong Kong competent authority exchanges correspondence with the competent authority of the partner jurisdiction informing them of the contact details of the responsible officers for EOI purposes. The contact details of the Hong Kong competent authority can also be found on the IRD's website (www.ird.gov.hk/eng/tax/dta_hkca.htm).

332. In light of Hong Kong's significant trade ties with the PRC and Japan (being the largest and the third-largest trading partner of Hong Kong

respectively), the Hong Kong competent authority has maintained close contact with the competent authorities of these jurisdictions ever since the EOI agreements with them were signed. Specifically, in the case of the PRC, the competent authorities of Hong Kong and the PRC have regular working meetings to deal with various issues arising from the implementation of their DTC. With more EOI agreements taking effect in the near future, Hong Kong's competent authority expects to maintain open communication channels with relevant competent authorities to ensure effective EOI.

333. The IRD has issued the following notes and circulars dealing with the interpretation and practical matters concerning exchange of information under DTCs. The IRD is currently working to extend these guidelines to TIEAs, in view of the enactment of the *Inland Revenue (Amendment) (No. 2) Ordinance 2013* on 19 July 2013. Moreover, a number of internal guidelines on processing EOI requests have also been issued, including (which are also in the process of being amended to cater for TIEAs):

- Departmental Interpretation and Practice Notes No. 47 on Exchange of Information under Comprehensive Double Taxation Agreements (CDTAs) issued in June 2010;
- Departmental Circular No. 11/2010 (Revised) on Exchange of Information under CDTAs issued in September 2012; and
- Departmental Circular No. 05/2012 on Preparing and Sending Exchange of Information Requests under CDTAs issued in July 2012.

Foreseeably relevant standard *(ToR C.1.1)*

334. The international standard for exchange of information envisages information exchange upon request to the widest possible extent. Nevertheless it does not allow "fishing expeditions," i.e. speculative requests for information that have no apparent nexus to an open inquiry or investigation. The balance between these two competing considerations is captured in the standard of "foreseeable relevance" which is included in Article 26(1) of the OECD *Model Taxation Convention* set out below:

> *The competent authorities of the contracting states shall exchange such information as is foreseeably relevant to the carrying out the provisions of this Convention or to the administration or enforcement of the domestic laws concerning taxes of every kind and description imposed on behalf of the contracting states or their political subdivisions or local authorities in so far as the taxation thereunder is not contrary to the Convention. The exchange of information is not restricted by Articles 1 and 2.*

335. Hong Kong's DTCs are patterned on the OECD *Model Taxation Convention* and its commentary as regards the scope of information that can be exchanged. All but three of Hong Kong's DTCs use the "foreseeably relevant" standard. Hong Kong's DTCs with Belgium (2003), Thailand (2005), and Vietnam (2008) use the term "as is necessary" in lieu of "as is foreseeably relevant". The term "as is necessary" is recognised in the commentary to Article 26 of the OECD *Model Taxation Convention* to allow for the same scope of exchange as does the term "foreseeably relevant".[40]

336. In practice, when receiving an EOI request, the Hong Kong authorities assess its validity against the EOI instrument and the *Disclosure Rules.* As mentioned in Part B of this report, the *Disclosure Rules* contain a "checklist" of items that an EOI request must contain to demonstrate that it meets the foreseeably relevant standard. Some of the requirements contained in the "checklist" can be waived (see more details in sections B.1.1 and B.1.2). During the three year period under review, Hong Kong has not declined to reply a request on the basis that it was not foreseeably relevant. The Hong Kong competent authority confirmed that to date it has never questioned whether the request from a treaty partner was a fishing expedition. Hong Kong has requested further clarification from the requesting jurisdiction in relation to approximately 23% of the EOI requests received concerning foreseeable relevance in a broad sense (including issues concerning the identification of the subject of the request, the type of tax, the period covered, missing enclosures). Those cases where clarification was requested are further detailed in section C.5 of this report.

In respect of all persons (ToR C.1.2)

337. For exchange of information to be effective it is necessary that a jurisdiction's obligation to provide information is not restricted by the residence or nationality of the person to whom the information relates or by the residence or nationality of the person in possession or control of the information requested. For this reason, the international standard for exchange of information envisages that exchange of information mechanisms will provide for exchange of information in respect of all persons.

338. All of Hong Kong's DTCs provide for EOI with respect to all persons. None of Hong Kong's agreements restricts the jurisdictional scope of the EOI provisions to certain persons, for example those considered resident in one of the contracting parties.

40. The word "necessary" in paragraph 1 of Article 26 of the 2003 OECD *Model Taxation Convention* was replaced by the phrase "foreseeably relevant" in the 2005 version. The commentary to Article 26 recognises that the term "necessary" allows for the same scope of exchange as does the term "foreseeably relevant".

Obligation to exchange all types of information (ToR C.1.3)

339. Jurisdictions cannot engage in effective exchange of information if they cannot exchange information held by financial institutions, nominees or persons acting in an agency or a fiduciary capacity. The OECD *Model Taxation Convention*, which is an authoritative source of the standards, stipulates that bank secrecy cannot form the basis for declining a request to provide information and that a request for information cannot be declined solely because the information is held by nominees or persons acting in an agency or fiduciary capacity or because the information relates to an ownership interest.

340. All but three of Hong Kong's DTCs include provisions akin to Article 26(5) of the OECD *Model Taxation Convention*, which provides that a contracting party may not decline to supply information solely because the information is held by a bank, other financial institution, nominee or person acting in an agency or a fiduciary capacity or because it relates to ownership interests in a person. Hong Kong's policy is to include Article 26(5) in all of its new agreements.

341. Although Hong Kong's agreements with Belgium, Thailand and Vietnam do not include such a provision, there are no limitations in Hong Kong's laws with respect to access to bank information, information held by nominees, and ownership and identity information. As of July 2011, there are no limitations in Belgium's laws with respect to access to bank information. There may be, however, such limitations in place in the domestic laws of Thailand and Vietnam. In these cases, the absence of a specific provision requiring exchange of bank information unlimited by bank secrecy may serve as a limitation on the EOI which can occur under the relevant DTC. It is noted that Hong Kong has contacted Thailand and Vietnam on a number of occasions, including in recent months to update the respective DTCs in line with the standard. Hong Kong should continue its efforts to renegotiate its older DTCs to include Article 26(5) of the OECD *Model Taxation Convention*. The Hong Kong authorities advise that as Hong Kong has never had bank secrecy laws, they would not refuse to respond to any request for banking information due to the absence of a provision akin to Article 26(5).

Absence of domestic tax interest (ToR C.1.4)

342. The concept of "domestic tax interest" describes a situation where a contracting party can only provide information to another contracting party if it has an interest in the requested information for its own tax purposes. An inability to provide information based on a domestic tax interest requirement is not consistent with the international standard. Contracting parties must use their information gathering measures even though invoked solely to obtain and provide information to the other contracting party.

343. All but three of Hong Kong's DTCs contain provisions akin to Article 26(4) of the OECD *Model Taxation Convention*, obliging the contracting parties to use information-gathering measures to exchange requested information without regard to a domestic tax interest. Hong Kong's DTCs with Belgium, Thailand and Vietnam do not contain such a provision. As explained in part B of this report, these agreements were signed prior to the legislative amendments abolishing Hong Kong's domestic tax interest requirement. Thus, the IRD's powers under the *Inland Revenue Ordinance* to access information pursuant to an EOI request are limited to there being a domestic tax interest in Hong Kong. As a result, these agreements do not meet the standard. It is noted that Hong Kong has contacted Belgium, Thailand, and Vietnam on a number of occasions, including in recent months to update the respective DTCs in line with the standard. Hong Kong should continue its efforts to renegotiate its older DTCs to include Article 26(4) of the OECD *Model Taxation Convention.* The Hong Kong authorities reported that, in June 2013, they received Vietnam's consent to update the EOI article in line with the standard and are arranging for the signing of a protocol to upgrade the EOI article. The Hong Kong authorities received feedback from the Belgian tax administration on the proposed upgrade to the EOI provision of their DTC in early August 2013. The Hong Kong authorities report that they are actively following this up with the Belgian authorities. In relation to Thailand, Hong Kong has contacted with the Thai competent authorities to update the EOI article in line with the international standard since 2010. However, a reply from Thailand in this regard is still pending.

344. During the period under review and prior to the 2010 amendment abolishing Hong Kong's domestic tax interest requirement, Hong Kong received two information requests from a treaty partner for which no domestic tax interest existed. Owing to the limitation in its information gathering powers at that time, the IRD was unable to reply to the requests as they concerned information in which the IRD had no domestic interest. It is noted that a protocol was subsequently signed with the treaty partner in question, which contains a provision akin to Article 26(4) of the OECD. As such, Hong Kong is now in a position to gather information upon the request of such treaty partner, despite the absence of a domestic tax interest.

Absence of dual criminality principles (ToR C.1.5)

345. The principle of dual criminality provides that assistance can only be provided if the conduct being investigated (and giving rise to an information request) would constitute a crime under the laws of the requested country if it had occurred in the requested country. In order to be effective, exchange of information should not be constrained by the application of the dual criminality principle.

346. There are no dual criminality requirements in Hong Kong's agreements for exchange of information in tax matters.

Exchange of information in both civil and criminal tax matters (ToR C.1.6)

347. Information exchange may be requested both for tax administration purposes and for tax prosecution purposes. The international standard is not limited to information exchange in criminal tax matters but extends to information requested for tax administration purposes (also referred to as "civil tax matters").

348. All of Hong Kong's exchange of information agreements provide for exchange of information in both civil and criminal tax matters.

349. There are no separate processes involved where an EOI request relates to criminal investigation. The Hong Kong competent authority does not anticipate any difficulties in providing effective EOI assistance where an EOI request relates to a criminal or a civil investigation.

Provide information in specific form requested (ToR C.1.7)

350. There are no restrictions in the exchange of information provisions in Hong Kong's DTCs that would prevent Hong Kong from providing information in a specific form, as long as this is consistent with its own administrative practices. During the period under review, Hong Kong was requested to provide authenticated copies of original documents in connection with some EOI requests it received. No difficulties have arisen with respect to this issue in practice.

In force (ToR C.1.8)

351. Exchange of information cannot take place unless a jurisdiction has exchange of information arrangements in force. Where exchange of information agreements have been signed the international standard requires that jurisdictions must take all steps necessary to bring them into force expeditiously.

352. Twenty-five[41] of the 29 agreements signed by Hong Kong are currently in force, of which 22 are to the international standard. Typically, these have taken less than a year from signing to come into force. Additionally, Hong

41. Austria; Belgium; Brunei; China, People's Republic of; the Czech Republic; France; Hungary; Indonesia; Ireland; Japan; Jersey; Kuwait; Liechtenstein; Luxembourg; Malaysia; Malta; Mexico; The Netherlands; New Zealand; Portugal; Spain; Switzerland; Thailand; the United Kingdom; and Vietnam.

Kong reports that it has completed the ratification procedures for its DTC with Canada and is now awaiting Canada to finalise its procedures. Hong Kong's other agreements not yet in force were signed in 2013. It is recommended that Hong Kong continue to bring agreements into force expeditiously.

353. In Hong Kong, a signed tax treaty agreement needs to become a piece of the domestic legislation for it to be effective. The Chief Executive in Council must declare by an Order under section 49(1A) of the *Inland Revenue Ordinance* that the EOI agreement has been made to bring the agreement into effect. The ratification procedures are as follows: (1) approval by the Executive Council, (2) publication in the gazette, (3) tabling at the Legislative Council for negative vetting and commencement of the Order after the vetting period. Hong Kong would then inform the contracting party of the completion of its ratification procedures. Upon receipt of the same notification from the other contracting party, the agreement will enter into force and be effective in accordance with the provisions of the agreement. Generally, it takes less than one year for Hong Kong bringing signed agreements into force, depending also on the notification from the other contracting party.

Be given effect through domestic law (ToR C.1.9)

354. For exchange of information to be effective, the contracting parties must enact any legislation necessary to comply with the terms of the agreement.

355. All of Hong Kong's agreements which have been signed and ratified by both parties are in effect in Hong Kong. Each DTC is implemented as a piece of subsidiary legislation under Hong Kong's *Inland Revenue Ordinance* (s. 49). As detailed in sections A.1 and B.1 of this report, there are however some limitations in the availability of information in Hong Kong and access to information by Hong Kong authorities. Thus, Hong Kong cannot be considered to have given full effect to these arrangements through domestic law.

356. Moreover, there was one aspect of Hong Kong's EOI framework in place during the period under review that did not fully meet the international standard which has been redressed recently by *Inland Revenue (Amendment) (No. 2) Ordinance 2013*. Under Hong Kong's previous framework (previously summarised in the *Disclosure Rules* and the Departmental Interpretation and Practice Notes No. 47 of June 2010), Hong Kong's competent authority was unable to exchange any information that preceded the effective date of the EOI agreement. By way of example, under the old framework, Hong Kong was not be able to provide its EOI partners with a copy of an agreement that had been executed before the treaty's effective date, even though it conferred rights and obligations in relation to subsequent periods covered by the EOI agreement. Similarly, a signature card or a statement concerning the opening

or operation of a bank account that pre-dated the effective date of the EOI agreement, but which referred to a bank account that was still being operated by a taxpayer, could not be exchanged with a treaty partner.

357. Effective as of 19 July 2013, Hong Kong amended the *Disclosure Rules* to ensure that information that precedes the effective date of an agreement can be exchanged, provided that such information relates to a taxable period following the EOI agreement's effective date. Hong Kong should monitor the application of its new legislation to ensure that information is exchanged in accordance with the minimum standard under the OECD Model TIEA.

358. The Hong Kong authorities report that they did not receive any requests during the period under review that referred to information that preceded the effective date of the relevant EOI agreement but which related to a taxable period following the EOI agreement effective date. The Hong Kong authorities also report that with effect from 19 July 2013, they have effectively exchanged information which preceded the effective date of the EOI instrument where it related to a taxable period covered by the EOI agreement.

Determination and factors underlying recommendations

Phase 1 determination	
The element is in place.	
Factors underlying recommendations	**Recommendations**
Three of Hong Kong's 29 DTCs do not provide for effective exchange of information. Hong Kong is actively pursuing the renegotiation of these DTCs.	Hong Kong should continue its efforts to renegotiate its agreements as necessary so that they provide for effective exchange of information.

Phase 2 rating	
Largely Compliant	
Factors underlying recommendations	**Recommendations**
Hong Kong's legal framework in force during the period under review prevented the exchange of information that preceded the effective date of the EOI agreement, although no requests were received during the period under review that could not be answered due to this limitation.	Hong Kong should monitor the application of its new legislation to ensure that information that precedes the effective date of the agreement can be exchanged, where it relates to a taxable period subsequent to the effective date of the EOI agreement.

C.2. Exchange-of-information mechanisms with all relevant partners

> The jurisdictions' network of information exchange mechanisms should cover all relevant partners.

359. Ultimately, the international standard requires that jurisdictions exchange information with all relevant partners, meaning those partners who are interested in entering into an information exchange arrangement. Agreements cannot be concluded only with counterparties without economic significance. If it appears that a jurisdiction is refusing to enter into agreements or negotiations with partners, in particular ones that have a reasonable expectation of requiring information from that jurisdiction in order to properly administer and enforce its tax laws it may indicate a lack of commitment to implement the standards.

360. Hong Kong has significantly expanded its network of EOI instruments in recent years. It has signed 26 agreements (Austria, Brunei, Canada, the PRC, the Czech Republic, France, Guernsey, Hungary, Indonesia, Ireland, Italy, Japan, Jersey, Kuwait, Liechtenstein, Luxembourg, Malaysia, Malta, Mexico, the Netherlands, New Zealand, Portugal, Qatar, Spain, Switzerland and the United Kingdom) that provide for effective EOI in tax matters in accordance with the international standard, of which 22 are in force. These agreements are with counterparties which represent:

- 8 of its major trading partners (the PRC, Japan, Malaysia, the United Kingdom, Switzerland, France, Italy and the Netherlands);
- 25 of the 119 Global Forum Member jurisdictions; and
- 16 of the 34 OECD member economies.

361. One of Hong Kong's agreements with a major trading partner (Italy) is not yet in force. The DTCs entered into with Canada, Guernsey and Qatar are also not yet in force. It is recommended that Hong Kong continue to work with these jurisdictions to bring these agreements into force expeditiously. It is noted, however, all EOI agreements that are not yet in force were signed less than a year ago.

362. Hong Kong currently has 10 treaty negotiations in various stages of progress. In addition, it is involved in renegotiating its existing DTCs that are not to the standard. In all cases, Hong Kong expects that the outcome will be EOI provisions to the international standard.

363. Comments were sought from Global Forum member jurisdictions in the course of the preparation of this report. A number of jurisdictions informed the assessment team that they approached Hong Kong to express interest in entering into a TIEA, but Hong Kong offered instead to negotiate a

DTC containing the internationally agreed exchange of information standard, because Hong Kong's law at the time did not allow for entering into TIEAs.

364. Hong Kong law has been amended recently to cater for such standalone TIEAs. The Hong Kong authorities advise that with the recent amendments in Hong Kong's legal framework Hong Kong is now in a position to negotiate and conclude TIEAs with jurisdictions that approach Hong Kong to do so, and is already in negotiations with some jurisdictions for TIEAs. The negotiations with other jurisdictions that have approached Hong Kong have been scheduled or are in the process of being scheduled.

365. The international standard requires that a jurisdiction exchange information with all relevant partners, meaning those partners who are interested in entering into an information agreement. It is recommended that, in accordance with the standard, Hong Kong ensures that it enters into EOI agreements (regardless of their form) with all relevant partners.

366. Hong Kong has signed agreements with eight of its significant trading partners and has signed agreements with a number of other economically significant jurisdictions. Given Hong Kong's importance as a global finance centre, it is essential that its agreements with its relevant partners meet the international standard.

Determination and factors underlying recommendations

Phase 1 determination	
The element is in place, but certain aspects of the legal implementation of the element need improvement.	
Factors underlying recommendations	**Recommendations**
Hong Kong has 26 signed agreements (22 of which are currently in force) which provide for effective exchange of information.	Hong Kong should bring its existing agreements that do not meet the standard up to the standard.
Hong Kong has been approached by a number of jurisdictions to negotiate a TIEA. Hong Kong has recently amended its domestic laws to allow for exchange of information under TIEAs or other exchange of information arrangements.	Hong Kong should enter into agreements for exchange of information (regardless of their form) with all relevant partners, meaning those partners who are interested in entering into an information exchange arrangement with it.

Phase 2 rating
Partially Compliant

C.3. Confidentiality

> The jurisdictions' mechanisms for exchange of information should have adequate provisions to ensure the confidentiality of information received.

Information received: disclosure, use, and safeguards (ToR C.3.1)

367. Governments would not engage in information exchange without the assurance that the information provided would only be used for the purposes permitted under the exchange mechanism and that its confidentiality would be preserved. Information exchange instruments must therefore contain confidentiality provisions that spell out specifically to whom the information can be disclosed and the purposes for which the information can be used. In addition to the protections afforded by the confidentiality provisions of information exchange instruments, jurisdictions with tax systems generally impose strict confidentiality requirements on information collected for tax purposes.

368. All EOI articles in Hong Kong's DTCs have confidentiality provisions modelled on Article 26(2) of the OECD *Model Taxation Convention.* Hong Kong's EOI agreements are part of Hong Kong's domestic law (*Inland Revenue Ordinance* s. 49).

369. The confidentiality provisions of Hong Kong's DTCs are backed by general confidentiality provisions in Hong Kong's domestic tax legislation. The *Inland Revenue Ordinance* provides that except in the performance of his or her duties under that ordinance, an officer of the Inland Revenue Department is obliged to preserve and aid in preserving secrecy with regard to all matters relating to the affairs of any taxpayer coming to his or her knowledge (s. 4). Section 49 provides that for the purposes of Hong Kong's DTCs, the obligations as to secrecy imposed by section 4 do not prevent the disclosure to any authorised officer of the government with which the DTC is made. Breach of confidentiality provisions by officers of the Inland Revenue Department is subject to a fine of HKD 50 000 (EUR 4 936) (s. 81).

All other information exchanged (ToR C.3.2)

370. The confidentiality provisions in Hong Kong's exchange of information agreements and domestic law do not draw a distinction between information received in response to requests and information forming part of the requests themselves. As such, these provisions apply equally to all requests for such information, background documents to such requests, and any other document reflecting such information, including communications between the requesting and requested jurisdictions and communications within the tax authorities of either jurisdiction.

Ensuring confidentiality in practice

371. Confidentiality is protected in Hong Kong by ensuring that all exchanges of information are made or received through the competent authority and by ensuring that the administrative processes for obtaining and collating information are delegated to a restricted number of tax officers. These officers are all employed within the IRD.

372. Access to premises is secured in the IRD. The Tax Treaty Section and other units involved in EOI are housed in one building, the Revenue Tower. Access by members of the public is restricted.

373. Information received from and provided to a treaty partner in connection with an EOI request is treated as strictly confidential and handled with care. The IRD has developed specific rules and guidelines to safeguard the confidentiality of information exchanged under an EOI arrangement. The guidelines on confidentiality and handling of EOI requests remind all officers involved in EOI of their confidentiality duty and the steps to be taken when handling requests.

374. Incoming EOI requests are marked with a "confidential" stamp, inserted in a confidential envelope and transmitted by hand to the case officers. All documentation relating to the processing of a request is kept in specific folders maintained for each request: the master folder (maintained by the Tax Treaty Section) and the unit folder (maintained by the unit that is assisting in the information gathering). Officers dealing with the request are not allowed to make or retain copies of documents unless the documents contain information in which Hong Kong has a domestic tax interest. Folders are kept in a cabinet under lock. After the completion of the answers to the requests, the master folder and the unit folder are kept by the Tax Treaty Section in a locked cabinet.

375. The access rights to Hong Kong's EOI database, the EOI Register, are also restricted to officers working in the Tax Treaty Section.

Notices for the production of information

376. To reply to an EOI request, the Hong Kong authorities may be required to gather information from subject persons or third parties who hold the information or documents (see Part B of this report). For this purpose, the authorities need to issue a notice to produce such information or documents.

377. The Hong Kong authorities have issued templates concerning the content of the formal notices issued in connection with EOI requests. The formal notice issued to third parties generally includes the following minimum information: *(i)* a reference to the access powers provided under the *Inland Revenue Ordinance*; *(ii)* a general description of the information

requested; *(iii)* the time limit to produce the information; *(iv)* a detailed list of the information requested; *(v)* a reference to the sanctions provided under the *Inland Revenue Ordinance* for failure to comply with the formal notice; and *(vi)* the name of the subject person for identification purposes when the information holder is not the subject person. If the case involves domestic tax interest, the formal notice will show the type of Hong Kong domestic tax. Where the case involves overseas tax, the IRD will omit the tax type from the formal notice.

378. The Model Convention, upon which the EOI agreements of Hong Kong are based, states as a basic proposition that any information received by a jurisdiction in the context of EOI must be treated as confidential or secret, and "*may be disclosed only to persons or authorities (including courts and administrative bodies) in the jurisdiction of the Contracting Party concerned with the assessment or collection of, the enforcement or prosecution in respect of, or the determination of appeals in relation to, the taxes covered by this Agreement. Such persons or authorities shall use such information only for such purposes. They may disclose the information in public court proceedings or judicial decisions.*"

379. As a matter of practicality, it is accepted that a requested jurisdiction needs to disclose to the information holder the minimum information contained in an EOI request necessary to enable the holder to locate the requested information and respond to the notice. The type and amount of information to be disclosed depends on the circumstances of each case, including, for example, the type or form of information requested, and the person from whom the information is sought. Therefore, the acceptable amount of information disclosed will differ on a case-by-case basis. The notices to produce information issued by the Hong Kong authorities disclose the minimum information necessary to enable the information holder to locate the requested information and respond to the notice.

380. The subject person has 14 days to request a copy of the information that the Commissioner of Inland Revenue intends to disclose to the requesting government. The subject person is not provided with a copy of the actual EOI request.

Provision of information to the FIU

381. The international standard is clear in that information relating to a request for information – whether received in response to a request or provided as part of making the request – is confidential and can only be disclosed to certain, specified persons or authorities (or, where the agreement provides, with the consent of the other party) and for specified purposes.

382. Pursuant to the *Organized and Serious Crimes Ordinance* (Cap. 455), any person in Hong Kong, including IRD officers, are obliged to report AML/CFT suspicious transactions to the JFIU (s. 25A). Hong Kong's legal definition of money laundering is broad, encompassing money linked to any indictable offence in Hong Kong, including tax evasion. The handling of proceeds or property from overseas tax evasion is also considered to be money laundering under Hong Kong law. The IRD is, therefore, obliged to report any suspicion or evidence of tax evasion to the JFIU.

383. The Hong Kong authorities report that IRD officers would not report suspicious transactions to the JFIU if such information is received by Hong Kong's competent authority from other competent authorities under an EOI request. The Hong Kong authorities consider that IRD officers are bound by the confidentiality provisions governing all Hong Kong's EOI agreements and that these confidentiality provisions prevail over the IRD's obligation to disclose information under the *Organized and Serious Crimes Ordinance* (Cap. 455). The IRD's interpretation in this regard is formalised in its internal guidelines (i.e. DIPN 47 of June 2010), which provides that the confidentiality provisions of the Comprehensive Double Taxation Agreements create obligations under international law and these provisions take precedence over any domestic rules that permit disclosure to persons not referred to in the confidentiality provisions. The IRD also reports that no information received from a foreign competent authority pursuant to an EOI request has ever been reported to the JFIU.

384. It is noted, however, that under Hong Kong's legal system treaties do not specifically override domestic law where there is a conflict between the two. Any conflict will be resolved in accordance with statutory interpretation rules. There may be a conflict between the IRD's obligations under Organized and Serious Crimes Ordinance (Cap. 455) and under Hong Kong's EOI agreements. It is recommended that Hong Kong clarify its laws to make it clear that the IRD is not obliged to disclose information contained in an EOI request received from a treaty partner and the IRD will only disclose such information to the JFIU if it is duly authorised to do so under the relevant EOI agreement. Nevertheless, it is noted that the IRD's practice is not to disclose to the JFIU any information received by Hong Kong's competent authority from other competent authorities under an EOI request.

385. Furthermore, the Hong Kong authorities advise that Hong Kong is prepared to adopt in its new tax treaties where appropriate an EOI article based on the 2012 update of the OECD Model concerning the use of information exchanged for non-tax purposes (i.e. "notwithstanding the foregoing, information received by a Contracting State may be used for other purposes when such information may be used for such other purposes under the laws of both States and the competent authority of the supplying State authorises

such use") given the agreement of Hong Kong's legislature in this regard. This will provide the basis for Hong Kong to exchange information under an EOI request for non-tax purposes and the disclosure of information to the JFIU can then be made where relevant agreements authorise such disclosure and in accordance with the terms of those agreements.

Determination and factors underlying recommendations

Phase 1 determination
The element is in place.

Phase 2 rating
Compliant

C.4. Rights and safeguards of taxpayers and third parties

> The exchange of information mechanisms should respect the rights and safeguards of taxpayers and third parties.

Exceptions to requirement to provide information (ToR C.4.1)

386. The international standard allows requested parties not to supply information in response to a request in certain identified situations where an issue of trade, business or other secret may arise. Among other reasons, an information request can be declined where the requested information would disclose confidential communications protected by the attorney-client privilege. Attorney-client privilege is a feature of the legal systems of many jurisdictions.

387. The limits on information which must be exchanged under Hong Kong's DTCs mirror those provided for in the international standard. That is, information which is subject to legal privilege; would disclose any trade, business, industrial, commercial or professional secret or trade process; or would be contrary to public policy, is not required to be exchanged.

388. Communications between a client and an attorney or other admitted legal representative are, generally, only privileged to the extent that, the attorney or other legal representative acts in his or her capacity as an attorney or other legal representative. Where attorney-client privilege is more broadly defined it does not provide valid grounds on which to decline a request for EOI. As noted in part B.1 of this report, Hong Kong's attorney-client privilege only applies to communications between a client and an attorney to the extent that the attorney acts in his or her professional capacity as an attorney.

389. No issues in relation to the rights and safeguards of taxpayers and third parties have been encountered in practice, nor have they been raised by any of Hong Kong's EOI partners.

Determination and factors underlying recommendations

Phase 1 determination
The element is in place.

Phase 2 rating
Compliant

C.5. Timeliness of responses to requests for information

The jurisdiction should provide information under its network of agreements in a timely manner.

Responses within 90 days (ToR C.5.1)

390. In order for exchange of information to be effective it needs to be provided in a timeframe which allows tax authorities to apply the information to the relevant cases. If a response is provided but only after a significant lapse of time the information may no longer be of use to the requesting authorities. This is particularly important in the context of international co-operation as cases in this area must be of sufficient importance to warrant making a request.

391. There are no specific legal or regulatory requirements in place which would prevent Hong Kong responding to a request for information by providing the information requested or providing a status update within 90 days of receipt of the request.

392. It is the IRD's policy to endeavour to reply to all EOI requests within 90 days. Circulars and handbooks issued by the IRD stress this commitment. Moreover, they also state that all IRD officers should give priority to EOI requests and process them without delay. When the IRD is unable to provide the information within the 90-day period, the Hong Kong's competent authority will inform the requesting competent authority and explain the reasons for not being able to do so upon the expiry of that period.

393. Over the period 1 July 2009 to 30 June 2012, Hong Kong received a total of 61 requests for information from four treaty partners (6 requests were received in 2009 (from 1 July), 17 in 2010, 15 in 2011, and 23 in 2012 (to 30 June)). Most requests received by Hong Kong in the period under review were sent by one partner, Hong Kong's main trading partner, the PRC. The

organisational process, procedures and resources are the same for requests coming from any of Hong Kong's treaty partners.

394. Hong Kong counts each written request from an EOI partner as one EOI request even where more than one person is the subject of an inquiry and/or more than one piece of information is requested. Of the 61 incoming requests, Hong Kong was in a position to reply within 90 days in 75% of the cases and within 180 days in 85% of the cases. More details are included in the table below.

Table 1. Response times for requests received during the three-year review period

		Jul-Dec 2009		2010		2011		Jan-Jun 2012		Total	Average
		nr.	%	nr.	%	nr.	%	nr.	%	nr.	%
Total number of requests received*	(a+b+c+d+e+f)	6	100	17	100	15	100	23	100	61	100
Full response** ≤90 days		6	100	9	53	10	67	21	91	46	75
≤180 days (cumulative)		6	100	11	64	14	93	21	91	52	85
≤1 year (cumulative)	(a)	6	100	11	64	14	93	21	91	52	85
> 1 year	(b)	0	0	2	12	0	0	0	0	2	3
Declined for valid reasons	(c)	0	0	1	6	1	7	0	0	2	4
Requests withdrawn by the requesting jurisdiction	(d)	0	0	3	18	0	0	2	9	5	8
Failure to obtain and provide information requested	(e)	0	0	0	0	0	0	0	0	0	0
Requests still pending at the time of the on-site visit	(f)	0	0	0	0	0	0	0	0	0	0

* Hong Kong counts each written request from an EOI partner as one EOI request even where more than one person is the subject of an inquiry and/or more than one piece of information is requested.

** The time periods in this table are counted from the date of receipt of the request to the date on which the final and complete response was issued.

395. The Hong Kong authorities have systematically provided up-dates when requests could not be answered within the IRD's committed 90-day timeframe. 5 of the 6 requests that Hong Kong took between 90 and 180 days to reply were actually replied to on the 91st or the 92nd day, as earlier in the review period, Hong Kong adopted a three-month period as its target maximum response time. Earlier in the review period, there were two instances where Hong Kong did not manage to provide updates when the requested information could not be provided within 90 days. In one of the cases, Hong Kong has followed-up with the requesting jurisdiction after four months from the date of the request and, in the

second case, Hong Kong apologised to the peer after having received a reminder after one year from the initial request. Hong Kong did provide full responses in connection with these requests and the peer considered that the responses were timely. In all other cases, Hong Kong has provided status updates and the peers that provided input to the review confirmed that. Hong Kong has taken appropriate action to address the issue, putting in place an electronic tracking system to ensure that timely status updates are given in all cases.

396. Hong Kong took more than 180 days to reply to only two requests. Those requests required Hong Kong to provide a wide range of information (ownership information, detailed accounting records, banking information) covering several years and/or several taxpayers. In some instances, there were difficulties concerning the identification of the person that was the subject of the request and clarification was sought from the requesting jurisdiction. Hong Kong provided full answers to the requests.

397. The Hong Kong authorities reported that in only one case one of the items listed in the EOI request, i.e. a tax return, was not available at the time of reply, because the deadline for annual tax filing had not yet expired. In the reply to the requesting party, Hong Kong explained the issue and informed the requesting party when the tax return would be available. A few months later, the requesting party, acting on the information provided in the reply, lodged a fresh request for the outstanding information and Hong Kong was able to respond to the request fully.

398. Inputs from Hong Kong's EOI partners received in the course of the peer review reveals that they were satisfied with the timeliness and quality of the responses provided by Hong Kong. One significant partner also acknowledged the significant progress that Hong Kong has made in the last three years.

399. The Hong Kong competent authority has sought clarification from requesting parties.

- in five cases, the Hong Kong authorities reported that the EOI requests did not contain sufficient information on the identity of the subject person(s). In relation to some requests, several individuals in the database of the IRD were found to have the same name provided in the EOI request. In other cases, more than one company in the database was identified bearing either the same Chinese or English name provided by the requesting party. Additional information such as identification number, address, etc., had to be sought from the requesting party to identify the correct subject persons to which the EOI requests related;
- in 11 cases, the Hong Kong authorities reported that essential information, such as the foreseeably relevance of the information, period covered, tax type concerned, reason for waiver of notification, was omitted in the EOI request;

- in four cases, the Hong Kong authorities reported that confirmation was sought from requesting parties as to whether the issue of notification to the subject person would undermine the prospects of success of the investigation and/or frustrate the timely enforcement of the tax laws of the requesting party.

400. As a general rule, the Hong Kong competent authority sends a reminder to its EOI partners two months after it has sent a request for clarification. If it receives no response to the reminder after two months, it considers the case to be closed for internal purposes. However, if it subsequently receives a response from the requesting party, the case is then re-opened. In relation to 15 of the 20 cases, after receiving further information/confirmation from the requesting party, the Hong Kong competent authority proceeded to process the EOI request. In the remaining 5 cases, no response was received from the requesting party and the cases were marked internally as closed.

401. Hong Kong's EOI partners that provided comments for this review did not raise concerns in relation to the clarifications requested by Hong Kong. Moreover, the number of requests for clarification declined over the period of the review. The Hong Kong authorities consider that this is a positive result of having greater experience with EOI and closer relationships with their partners.

402. During the period under review, Hong Kong's competent authority has declined to respond to two EOI requests. The requests could not be answered because they were not in compliance with Hong Kong's legislation, which until March 2010 contained a domestic tax interest requirement (see section *C.1.4* of this report for more details). The domestic tax interest requirement was removed in relation to all agreements and protocols signed after March 2010.

403. Five requests were not pursued by the requesting jurisdiction after Hong Kong asked for clarification concerning the identification of the subject person, the foreseeable relevance of the request etc. (for more details see paragraph above detailing the requests for clarification made by Hong Kong).

Organisational process and resources (ToR C.5.2)

404. Hong Kong's legal and regulatory framework relevant to exchange of information for tax purposes is presided over by the Financial Services and the Treasury Bureau. Administration of the EOI under Hong Kong's treaty network is the responsibility of Hong Kong's competent authority, i.e. the Commissioner of Inland Revenue. Under the *Inland Revenue Ordinance,* the Commissioner, or his authorised representative, is empowered to obtain ownership, identity, accounting, or bank information for the purpose of responding to a specific request for EOI in tax matters (s. 51).

405. Hong Kong has adequate resources to exchange information effectively. There is sufficient professional staff with clear responsibility for processing requests and retrieving and obtaining the requested information. The staff members also possess the requisite expertise and have undergone training specific to international EOI. Comprehensive guidelines have been issued covering all relevant steps in the EOI process. Hong Kong has developed an electronic tracking system and responses to requests are properly monitored.

406. Hong Kong has developed practical experience with exchanging information in recent years. Most processes and procedures were developed during the years coinciding with the period under review. The great majority of requests received to date come from one EOI partner, the PRC, Hong Kong's main trading partner. Given the entry into force of a number of EOI agreements and the continuous expansion of Hong Kong's EOI network in recent years, the number of incoming EOI requests can be expected to increase.

Resources

Human Resources

407. Under all Hong Kong's EOI instruments, the Commissioner of Inland Revenue or his authorised representative is the competent authority of Hong Kong. The Commissioner has authorised his two Deputy Commissioners to act as his representatives.

408. The Deputy Commissioner of Inland Revenue (Technical) oversees the Tax Treaty Section which is responsible for all matters relating to international tax including EOI with treaty partners.

409. After receiving its first EOI request in February 2007, the IRD has built up its capacity in EOI and officers are gaining more exposure and experience in handling EOI requests. Resources have been substantially increased within the Tax Treaty Section to strengthen the capability to handle EOI requests. At present, the Tax Treaty Section comprises a total of 12 full-time staff (1 chief assessor, 4 senior assessors, 4 assessors, 2 taxation officers and 1 personal secretary). In April 2009, there were only two senior assessors in the section. With more EOI instruments coming into force, Hong Kong advised it will continue to closely monitor the need for additional staff.

410. In addition to the Tax Treaty Section, the professional officers ranked senior assessor or above in Unit 1 (Profits Tax), Unit 2 (Individuals Tax), Unit 4 (Investigations) and Headquarters Unit (Property Tax) are also involved in handling and processing EOI requests. All professional officers involved in EOI matters hold at least a bachelor's degree in related fields and/or professional qualifications in accounting, as well as having more than ten years' experience in tax administration.

411. Training has been arranged to enhance the professional competence of staff in handling EOI requests. Officers are nominated on a regular basis to attend overseas training courses on matters relating to tax treaties (including topics on EOI) organised by various organisations such as the OECD, the Study Group on Asian Tax Administration and Research and the Australian Taxation Office. Internal seminars are also conducted for all professional officers of the IRD.

Technical Resources

412. A computerised register (the EOI Register) has been developed to enable efficient and proper monitoring of the processing of EOI requests. The EOI Register is used to record and keep track of all incoming EOI requests. To ensure the confidentiality of information, access rights to the EOI Register are restricted to officers working in the Tax Treaty Section. The IRD has also issued detailed work procedures, staff handbooks and guidelines on maintaining the EOI register which must be followed by all officers involved.

413. To monitor EOI, three control reports, namely a management report, work-in-progress report and completion report are generated monthly for review by the designated officer (i.e. the Tax Treaty Section's chief assessor).

414. The management report shows the overall position of the requests being processed, including statistics on the number of requests received, requests under information gathering processes and requests completed. It also shows the name of the requesting jurisdiction.

415. The work-in-progress report provides a detailed breakdown of any cases not yet completed, including all relevant dates (e.g. date of valid request, date of issue of notification, date of issue of notice for information gathering) and the file movement of the Unit Folder. In particular, it also highlights those cases approaching the 90-day response time limit.

416. The completion report shows an analysis of the cases completed, including the number of requests completed, nature of information requested and exchanged and also the length of time for providing a response to a valid request.

417. These reports are management tools for monitoring the progress of an EOI request and also indicate whether an EOI request has been processed efficiently. If any case is noted as having fallen behind schedule, the Tax Treaty Section's chief assessor will instruct the officers in charge to expedite the progress and also provide guidance, where necessary, for remedial action. The chief assessor will also work to streamline the EOI procedures to improve their effectiveness.

Organisational Process

418. The organisational process for handling EOI requests is defined in detail in written procedures (including flowcharts, checklists, templates, step-by-step processing instructions) which are followed in practice. IRD's senior personnel closely monitor every stage of the process and the EOI Register sends automatic warnings by e-mail when a certain (internal/external) deliverable is due. Templates are available to facilitate the handling of incoming requests.

419. The organisational process, procedures and resources are the same for requests coming from any of Hong Kong's treaty partners. When an EOI request is received by the Hong Kong competent authority, the request is forwarded directly to the Tax Treaty Section. An assessor of the Tax Treaty Section inputs the particulars of the request into the EOI Register and examines whether the request meets the requirements specified in the relevant EOI agreement and the Disclosure Rules. Within seven working days, the assessor should be in a position to take one of the following actions:

- if the request meets the requirements of the treaty/Disclosure Rules, the assessor (after vetting by the assessor's senior officer and approval from the Deputy Commissioner of Inland Revenue) will send an acknowledgement letter to the requesting party and will then forward the case to an officer in the IRD's Unit(s) responsible for gathering the information;
- if the request is considered unclear or incomplete, the assessor will draft a letter requesting further clarification. The letter is vetted by the assessor's senior officer and approved by the Deputy Commissioner of Inland Revenue before it is sent;
- if the request is considered to be invalid, the assessor will draft a letter to the requesting party, setting out the reason(s) why the request is not valid (e.g. EOI instrument is not yet in force or does not cover a certain tax). The letter is vetted by the assessor's senior officer and approved by the Deputy Commissioner of Inland Revenue before it is sent.

420. Where information needed to respond a request is in the custody of the IRD, the case officer in charge is expected to access such information expeditiously and prepare a draft reply in a short time frame (approximately 30 days from the receipt of the request). In cases where information is held by another government department, a notice pursuant to s. 52 (1) of the *Inland Revenue Ordinance* is issued. Co-operation from another department is also expected within a short time frame and the case officer in charge is also expected to draft a reply within approximately 30 days.

421. When gathering information held by external parties (such as a bank, a service provider or the person that is the subject of the enquiry), the case officer issues a notice to the information holder requiring the information be provided with a prescribed time limit. Normally the time limit is 14 to 21 days, depending on the degree of accessibility of the information and the volume of documents involved. After receiving the information from the holder, the case officer prepares a draft reply to the request and provides it to the officer in charge in the Tax Treaty Section.

422. The case officer will also issue the notification to the person that is the subject of the request (i.e. in situations where it has not been waived). In situations where the Deputy Commissioner of Inland Revenue is satisfied that prior notification is likely to frustrate the timely enforcement of the tax laws of the requesting party, the notification will be issued by the assessor of the Tax Treaty Section when the response is finally approved and signed by the Deputy Commissioner of Inland Revenue. In situations where the Deputy Commissioner of the Inland Revenue is satisfied that notification is likely to undermine the prospects of success of the investigation by the requesting party, notification is waived.

423. All drafts answers prepared by the case officers are reviewed by an assessor and his/her senior officer in the Tax Treaty Section to ensure their adequacy and completeness. The responses are finally approved and signed by the Deputy Commissioner of Inland Revenue. Interim replies setting out the progress in replying to requests are sent if a final reply cannot be given in 90 days. Those interim replies are also approved and signed by the Deputy Commissioner of Inland Revenue.

Absence of unreasonable, disproportionate or unduly restrictive conditions on exchange of information (ToR C.5.3)

424. There are no laws or regulatory practices in Hong Kong that impose restrictive conditions on exchange of information.

Determination and factors underlying recommendations

Phase 1 determination
This element involves issues of practice that are assessed in the Phase 2 review. Accordingly no Phase 1 determination has been made.

Phase 2 rating
Compliant

Summary of Determinations and Factors Underlying Recommendations

Determination	Factors underlying recommendations	Recommendations
Jurisdictions should ensure that ownership and identity information for all relevant entities and arrangements is available to their competent authorities *(ToR A.1)*		
Phase 1 determination: The element is in place, but certain aspects of the legal implementation need improvement.	Nominees that are not subject to AML obligations (i.e. those other than lawyers or financial institutions) are not required to maintain ownership and identity information in respect of all persons for whom they act as legal owners.	An obligation should be established for all nominees to maintain relevant ownership information where they act as the legal owners on behalf of any other persons.
	While there are no share warrants to bearer in circulation at present, there are currently insufficient mechanisms in place that ensure the availability of information allowing for identification of their owners. The new *Companies Ordinance*, which has been enacted but is not yet in operation, repeals the power of a company to issue share warrants to bearer as of the day the ordinance becomes operative.	Hong Kong should continue to take necessary steps to ensure that robust mechanisms are in place to identify the owners of share warrants to bearer or eliminate companies' ability to issue such shares.

Determination	Factors underlying recommendations	Recommendations
Phase 1 determination: The element is in place, but certain aspects of the legal implementation need improvement *(continued).*	Not all trustees of private express trusts and foreign trusts are statutorily required to have information available on the identity of settlors and beneficiaries of trusts.	Hong Kong should ensure that information that identifies the settlors, trustees and beneficiaries of private express trusts and foreign trusts in respect of which a trustee is resident in Hong Kong, is available to its competent authority.
Phase 2 rating: Partially Compliant	In circumstances where Hong Kong trustees of private express trusts or foreign trusts are not Hong Kong financial institutions or lawyers, and the trust neither carries on business in Hong Kong nor derives income which is taxable in Hong Kong, there is no systematic monitoring by government authorities of whether the trustees maintain information or documents pertaining to the identification of settlors and beneficiaries of these trusts.	Hong Kong should monitor whether Hong Kong trustees of private express trusts and foreign trusts maintain information that identifies the settlors and beneficiaries in all cases.
Jurisdictions should ensure that reliable accounting records are kept for all relevant entities and arrangements *(ToR A.2)*		
Phase 1 determination: The element is in place.	Trustees of private express trusts and foreign trusts are only statutorily required to maintain accounting records where the trust is carrying on business in Hong Kong.	Hong Kong should ensure that trustees of private express trusts and foreign trusts maintain accounting records even where the trust is not carrying on business in Hong Kong.

Determination	Factors underlying recommendations	Recommendations
Phase 2 rating: Largely Compliant	In circumstances where Hong Kong trustees of private express trusts or foreign trusts are not Hong Kong financial institutions or lawyers, and the trust neither carries on business in Hong Kong nor derives income which is taxable in Hong Kong, there is no systematic monitoring by government authorities of whether accounting records or underlying documents are being maintained.	Hong Kong should monitor whether Hong Kong resident trustees keep accounting records in all cases that fully meet the international standards and that those records are kept for at least five years.
Banking information should be available for all account-holders *(ToR A.3)*		
Phase 1 determination: The element is in place.		
Phase 2 rating: Compliant		
Competent authorities should have the power to obtain and provide information that is the subject of a request under an exchange of information arrangement from any person within their territorial jurisdiction who is in possession or control of such information (irrespective of any legal obligation on such person to maintain the secrecy of the information) *(ToR B.1)*		
Phase 1 determination: The element is in place.	Hong Kong has a domestic tax interest requirement with respect to 3 of its 29 exchange of information partners. Hong Kong's competent authority has contacted the relevant exchange of information partners on a number of occasions to update the respective EOI provisions in line with the standard.	Hong Kong should continue its efforts to ensure that its competent authority has the power to obtain all relevant information with respect to all exchange of information agreements (regardless of their form).
Phase 2 rating: Compliant		
The rights and safeguards (e.g. notification, appeal rights) that apply to persons in the requested jurisdiction should be compatible with effective exchange of information *(ToR B.2)*		
Phase 1 determination: The element is in place.		
Phase 2 rating: Compliant		

Determination	Factors underlying recommendations	Recommendations
Exchange of information mechanisms should allow for effective exchange of information *(ToR C.1)*		
Phase 1 determination: The element is in place.	Three of Hong Kong's 29 DTCs do not provide for effective exchange of information. Hong Kong is actively pursuing the renegotiation of these DTCs.	Hong Kong should continue its efforts to renegotiate its agreements as necessary so that they provide for effective exchange of information.
Phase 2 rating: Largely Compliant	Hong Kong's legal framework in force during the period under review prevented the exchange of information that preceded the effective date of the EOI agreement, although no requests were received during the period under review that could not be answered due to this limitation.	Hong Kong should monitor the application its new legislation to ensure that information that precedes the effective date of the agreement can be exchanged, where it relates to a taxable period subsequent to the effective date of the EOI agreement.
The jurisdictions' network of information exchange mechanisms should cover all relevant partners *(ToR C.2)*		
Phase 1 determination: The element is in place, but certain aspects of the legal implementation need improvement.	Hong Kong has 26 signed agreements (22 of which are currently in force) which provide for effective exchange of information.	Hong Kong should bring its existing agreements that do not meet the standard up to the standard.
	Hong Kong has been approached by a number of jurisdictions to negotiate a TIEA. Hong Kong has recently amended its domestic laws to allow for exchange of information under TIEAs or other exchange of information arrangements.	Hong Kong should enter into agreements for exchange of information (regardless of their form) with all relevant partners, meaning those partners who are interested in entering into an information exchange arrangement with it.
Phase 2 rating: Partially Compliant		
The jurisdictions' mechanisms for exchange of information should have adequate provisions to ensure the confidentiality of information received*(ToR C.3)*		
Phase 1 determination: The element is in place.		
Phase 2 rating: Compliant		

Determination	Factors underlying recommendations	Recommendations
The exchange of information mechanisms should respect the rights and safeguards of taxpayers and third parties *(ToR C.4)*		
Phase 1 determination: The element is in place.		
Phase 2 rating: Compliant		
The jurisdiction should provide information under its network of agreements in a timely manner *(ToR C.5)*		
This element involves issues of practice that are assessed in the Phase 2 review. Accordingly no Phase 1 determination has been made.		
Phase 2 rating: Compliant		

Annex 1: Jurisdiction's Response to the Report[42]

The Hong Kong delegation wishes to express sincere gratitude for the thorough and hard work of the assessment team throughout the Peer Review exercise.

Positive Outcome of the Peer Review

1. Hong Kong is very pleased to note that both Phase 1 and Phase 2 reviews have duly recognized Hong Kong's commitment to meeting the international standards on tax transparency. The Phase 1 review concludes that Hong Kong has adequate legal and regulatory framework in place to facilitate effective exchange of information. Hong Kong welcomes the outcome of the Phase 2 review which confirms that Hong Kong has gained practical experience with exchanging information over the years. The review has recognized that Hong Kong's competent authority (i.e. the Inland Revenue Department) is well prepared to deal with increasing demand and has adequate resources to exchange information effectively. In particular, the review noted that the Inland Revenue Department has the capability to respond effectively to exchange of information requests from our treaty partners by exercising powers to obtain bank, ownership, identity and accounting information as provided in the law. Enforcement provisions are also in place to ensure compliance with relevant obligations to maintain ownership and identity information through a combination of tax law, company law and regulatory laws. Our treaty partners consider Hong Kong to be an efficient and co-operative partner. They are satisfied with the timeliness and the content of the responses received.

42. This Annex presents the jurisdiction's response to the review report and shall not be deemed to represent the Global Forum's views.

Timely Follow-up on Necessary Enhancements

2. Hong Kong has all along been supportive of the international efforts to enhance tax transparency and combat tax evasion. Since the Phase 1 peer review, Hong Kong has actively pursued the recommendations put forward by the Peer Review Group, especially in putting in place a legal framework for tax information exchange agreements ("TIEAs") and enhancing the legal and regulatory regime governing the availability of ownership and identity information.

3. Specifically, Hong Kong's legislature passed the new Companies Ordinance in July 2012, which repeals the power of a company to issue share warrants to bearer. The Anti-money Laundering and Counter-Terrorist Financing (Financial Institutions) Ordinance has been in operation since 1 April 2012. All these further ensure the availability of ownership and identity information in Hong Kong.

4. Hong Kong's legislature also enacted in July 2013 the new legislation that enables the competent authority to enter into standalone TIEAs. Since 19 July 2013, both forms of information exchange instrument, namely comprehensive avoidance of double taxation agreement ("CDTA") and TIEA are available. Hong Kong will continue to pursue TIEA negotiations with relevant partners, including those with the United States, Denmark, the Faroes, Greenland, Iceland, Norway and Sweden.

5. Meanwhile, we will continue to expand our network of CDTAs. Up till now, Hong Kong has signed 29 CDTAs, 25 of which are already in force. Hong Kong has put in place requisite resources to ensure requests for exchange of information are handled in an effective and efficient manner. It is encouraging that our effort has been affirmed by both our treaty partners and the assessment team. As recognized in the report, Hong Kong processed a total of 61 requests during the review period of 1 July 2009 to 30 June 2012. Since then, Hong Kong has received 27 new requests for exchange of information from a wider range of treaty partners, including Belgium, Hungary, Indonesia, Japan, Luxembourg, the Netherlands, New Zealand, Thailand and the United Kingdom. Hong Kong will continue to ensure that all future requests are processed in accordance with the standard of the Global Forum.

Continued Support for International Tax Co-operation

6. Hong Kong is aware of growing aspirations of the international community on tax transparency and co-operation. In the years ahead, we will strive to expand our network of CDTAs and TIEAs with all

relevant partners to facilitate information exchange. We will continue to implement exchange of information arrangements effectively in the light of experience gained through CDTAs and TIEAs and the latest international developments.

7. The Hong Kong Government attaches great importance to the Peer Review. We will do our best to address the recommendations made in the report.

Annex 2: List of All Exchange-of-Information Mechanisms in Force

No.	Jurisdiction	Type of EOI agreement	Date signed	Date In force
1	Austria	Double Tax Convention (DTC) DTC Protocol	25 May 2010 25 June 2012	01 Jan 2011 3 Jul 2013
2	Belgium	DTC	10 Dec 2003	07 Oct 2004
3	Brunei	DTC	20 Mar 2010	19 Dec 2010
4	Canada	DTC	11 Nov 2012	---
5	People's Republic of China	DTC (Protocol to the 2006 Treaty)	27 May 2010	20 Dec 2010
6	Czech Republic	DTC	06 Jun 2011	24 Jan 2012
7	France	DTC	21 Oct 2010	01 Dec 2011
8	Guernsey	DTC	22 April 2013	---
9	Hungary	DTC	12 May 2010	23 Feb 2011
10	Indonesia	DTC	23 Mar 2010	28 Mar 2012
11	Ireland	DTC	22 Jun 2010	10 Feb 2011
12	Italy	DTC	14 Jan 2013	---
13	Japan	DTC	09 Nov 2010	14 Aug 2011
14	Jersey	DTC	15 Feb 2012	3 Jul 2013
15	Kuwait	DTC	13 May 2010	24 July 2013
16	Liechtenstein	DTC	12 Aug 2010	08 Jul 2011
17	Luxembourg	DTC DTC Protocol	02 Nov 2007 11 Nov 2010	20 Jan 2009 17 Aug 2011
18	Malaysia	DTC	25 Apr 2012	28 Dec 2012
19	Malta	DTC	8 Nov 2011	18 Jul 2012
20	Mexico	DTC	18 Jun 2012	7 Mar 2013

No.	Jurisdiction	Type of EOI agreement	Date signed	Date In force
21	Netherlands	DTC	22 Mar 2010	24 Oct 2011
22	New Zealand	DTC	01 Dec 2010	9 Nov 2011
23	Portugal	DTC	22 Mar 2011	3 Jun 2012
24	Qatar	DTC	13 May 2013	---
25	Spain	DTC	01 Apr 2011	13 Apr 2012
26	Switzerland	DTC Updated DTC	06 Dec 2010 4 Oct 2011	--- 15 Oct 2012
27	Thailand	DTC	07 Sep 2005	07 Dec 2005
28	United Kingdom	DTC	21 Jun 2010	20 Dec 2010
29	Vietnam	DTC	16 Dec 2008	12 Aug 2009

Annex 3: List of All Laws, Regulations and Other Relevant Material

Commercial Laws

Business Registration Ordinance

Companies Ordinance

New Companies Ordinance (not yet in effect)

Conveyancing and Property Ordinance

Estate Agents Ordinance

Insurance Companies Ordinance

Limited Partnerships Ordinance

Mandatory Provident Fund Schemes (General) Regulation

Occupational Retirement Schemes Ordinance

Partnerships Ordinance

Registered Trustees Incorporation Ordinance

Securities and Futures Ordinance

Trustee Ordinance

Taxation Laws

Inland Revenue Ordinance

Inland Revenue (Disclosure of Information) Rules

Inland Revenue (Amendment) (No. 2) Ordinance 2013

Banking Laws

Banking Ordinance

Anti-Money Laundering Laws

Anti-Money Laundering and Counter-Terrorist Financing (Financial Institutions) Ordinance

Drug Trafficking (Recovery of Proceeds) Ordinance

Organized and Serious Crimes Ordinance

United Nations (Anti-Terrorism Measures) Ordinance

Anti-Money Laundering Guidelines

Hong Kong Monetary Authority's guidelines and supplements

Securities and Futures Commission's guidelines

Office of the Commissioner of Insurance's guidelines

The Hong Kong Law Society's practice direction

Estate Agents Authority's practice circulars

The Hong Kong Institute of Certified Public Accountants Advisory Legal Bulletin & Codes of Ethics

Precious stones and precious metals dealers: advisory guidelines

The Hong Kong Institute of Chartered Secretaries' advisory guidelines

Guidelines issued by Narcotics Division

Other Laws

Basic Law

Legal Practitioners Ordinance

Personal Data (Privacy) Ordinance

Professional Accountants Ordinance

Annex 4: List of Authorities Interviewed

Commissioner of Inland Revenue (competent authority), deputy commissioners and representatives, Hong Kong's Inland Revenue Department

Secretary for Financial Services and the Treasury and representatives, Financial Services and the Treasury Bureau

Representatives, Business Registration Office

Representatives, Companies Registry

Representative, Department of Justice

Representatives, Securities and Futures Commission

Representatives, The Hong Kong Monetary Authority

Representatives, The Law Society of Hong Kong

Representatives, The Hong Kong Institute of Certified Public Accountants

Representatives, The Hong Kong Trustees' Association

Representative, The Hong Kong Institute of Chartered Secretaries

ORGANISATION FOR ECONOMIC CO-OPERATION AND DEVELOPMENT

The OECD is a unique forum where governments work together to address the economic, social and environmental challenges of globalisation. The OECD is also at the forefront of efforts to understand and to help governments respond to new developments and concerns, such as corporate governance, the information economy and the challenges of an ageing population. The Organisation provides a setting where governments can compare policy experiences, seek answers to common problems, identify good practice and work to co-ordinate domestic and international policies.

The OECD member countries are: Australia, Austria, Belgium, Canada, Chile, the Czech Republic, Denmark, Estonia, Finland, France, Germany, Greece, Hungary, Iceland, Ireland, Israel, Italy, Japan, Korea, Luxembourg, Mexico, the Netherlands, New Zealand, Norway, Poland, Portugal, the Slovak Republic, Slovenia, Spain, Sweden, Switzerland, Turkey, the United Kingdom and the United States. The European Union takes part in the work of the OECD.

OECD Publishing disseminates widely the results of the Organisation's statistics gathering and research on economic, social and environmental issues, as well as the conventions, guidelines and standards agreed by its members.

OECD PUBLISHING, 2, rue André-Pascal, 75775 PARIS CEDEX 16
(23 2013 73 1 P) ISBN 978-92-64-20612-0 – No. 60981 2013-01